COPING
WITH

Compulsive
Behavior

COPING WITH

MAY 2 9 1996

Compulsive

Behavior

Margot Webb

THE ROSEN PUBLISHING GROUP, INC./NEW YORK

Published in 1994 by The Rosen Publishing Group, Inc.
29 East 21st Street, New York, NY 10010

First Edition

Webb, Margot.
    Copng with compulsive behavior / Margot Webb.
    Includes bibliographical references and index.
    ISBN 0-8239-1604-9
    1. Compulsive behavior—Juvenile literature. [Compulsive
    behavior.] I. Title.
    RC533.W43
    616.85'227—dc20   93-29403
                                                    CIP
                                                    AC

Manufactured in the United States of America

ABOUT THE AUTHOR ◇

Margot Webb has been a teacher and a counselor to children in California, in the Los Angeles area. In these capacities she came to know these young people well, many of whom came from gang-infested neighborhoods.

Born in Germany during the Holocaust, Mrs. Webb managed to escape with her parents in 1939, but the rest of her family died in Auschwitz.

Settling in California, Mrs. Webb studied opera and was fortunate enough to appear in a few productions. She entered the University of Southern California with the express purpose of continuing her musical career but was married instead. She and her husband, a Hindu from India, lived for three years in Bombay before returning to the United States.

Widowed, she first began to teach. She then took a master's degree in counseling and began work on a doctorate at the University of Southern California. Remarried now, Mrs. Webb lives with her husband, an editor, in the Los Padres Mountain region, fairly close to Los Angeles.

Contents

Introduction

Senior rehearsal for graduation from Fern High School was over. Susan stood next to Robin in the afternoon heat.

"I think we're all glad this is finished," she told Robin, "I thought I'd faint during Mr. Bates's directions."

Robin laughed. "That's right! He just loves to tell people where to sit, when to stand, how to march—never mind, it's over. I'm so thirsty. Want to go for a Coke?"

"I have a better idea," Susan answered. "Let's go to my house where it's air-conditioned and have our Cokes there."

"Great!" Robin said.

The girls walked through the schoolyard to the street shimmering in the heat.

When they arrived at the house, Susan took out the key, explaining that her parents both worked. She took a tissue out of her purse and turned the doorknob.

Robin wondered out loud why Susan had done that. "Oh, my hands were sticky from the heat and I thought the doorknob would slide around." Susan's laugh sounded forced and brittle.

The girls went into the cool house. Although Robin had been there before, she was amazed anew at the beauty and orderliness of each room. So unlike her parents' cozy lived-in house full of books, magazines, and the ever-noisy presence of her younger brother.

Susan led the way to the all-white kitchen and indicated

a bar stool at the counter. Robin gratefully perched on it and watched Susan wash her hands at the sink. No sooner had she dried them than she ran the water and washed her hands again. The third time this happened, Robin burst out, "Hey, Susan, you're not performing surgery, you're just getting us a Coke."

Susan blushed uncomfortably and turned toward the refrigerator. She had a clean paper towel in her hand and wiped the door handle with it before opening it. She reached inside for two Cokes.

Robin stretched her hand out: Her thirst was about to be quenched. But Susan pulled away. "Don't drink out of the can," she commanded. "I'll get glasses and ice." Robin shrugged. Her thirst was beginning to be replaced with irritation.

Susan began to wash the clean glasses she had taken from the cupboard. When she used a fresh paper towel to open the refrigerator again, and still another to push the lever for ice cubes, Robin jumped off her stool. She put her arms around Susan and asked gently, "What on earth is going on?"

Susan burst into tears.

"I can't help it. Something inside makes me do everything this way. I hate it . . . but I have to do it."

"Do what?" Robin looked puzzled.

"I have to clean everything three times, never touch a doorknob, and make sure NOTHING is ever spilled in this whiter than white kitchen." Her voice was bitter. Susan put her head in her hands and began to sob in earnest.

"Why don't you just stop doing all those things?" Robin said. "After all, nobody's demanding it."

"You don't understand!" Susan became more agitated by the minute. "I HAVE to do it, or I'll be punished."

"Punished? By whom? Do your parents abuse you?" Robin drew closer to Susan.

"Abuse me? Of course not. My parents don't even know I do these things. I try to hide my obsession. I *will* be punished, but not by my parents. The punishment will come from me if I don't wash everything three times— showering, washing my hair, making my bed, and sometimes doing my calculus homework, all three times."

"What sort of punishment do you expect from yourself?" Robin whispered, trying to calm her friend.

"I don't know. That's just the trouble. I only know that something terrible will happen."

"To you?"

"*I don't know*, I told you. I realize it's irrational, but I can't take the chance. I'm stuck, that's all."

Susan handed the shiny glass of Coke to Robin and picked hers up with a paper towel.

The girls sipped in silence in the cool, clean kitchen, each engrossed in their own unhappy thoughts.

Susan was a victim of compulsive behavior. She forced herself to perform repetitive acts. Something in her background had made her a prisoner of her own mind. These acts were self-imposed—no one told her she had to behave that way. But a larger fear, a fear of an unknown punishment, drove her on.

Coping with compulsive behavior and finally ending it is possible. It is difficult to give up compulsive habits, but you can begin to peer at the fear "monster" you yourself created.

If you are suffering from any type of compulsion, you need help. That's what this book is all about: getting help and learning to cope.

First of all, you need to understand what compulsive behavior is all about and the possible reasons for it.

As always, the more you know about what is troubling you, the easier it is to find the kind of help you need.

Susan's first step was to confide in her friend Robin. Once the silence was broken, it was probably easier for Susan to talk about it again, perhaps even with others.

It's a long road of work and talk and courage to become acquainted with your inner self, to move from the prison of compulsive behavior to a free and happy life.

It can be done—and you can do it!

CHAPTER 1

What Is Compulsive Behavior?

Compulsive behavior comes from somewhere deep inside you. It pushes you to perform certain acts. It is strictly self-imposed.

Is it uncomfortable? Indeed it is! You *have* to do certain things for fear that you may be punished or lose your sight or even die. A big part of you, your intellect, tells you that compulsion is not based on reality. For example, Susan probably seemed ridiculous to you. To her, however, it was a burden she carried in each and every activity.

You know, at some level, that your compulsive behavior is forced on you by yourself. You think you can stop at any time. After all, no one knows you blink your eyes ten times whenever a teacher asks you a question. You can stop, you tell yourself.

Then why is your heart pounding as you even contemplate stopping? Why are your eyes blinking rapidly?

"No," you tell yourself—"I can't stop today, but maybe tomorrow will be my lucky day."

Compulsion is compelling. If you don't do what your inner self tells you to do, who knows what may happen? So you keep on blinking to ward off whatever terrible thing might happen.

You may wonder how your particular compulsion started. After all, you weren't born blinking your eyes constantly, or washing already clean glasses three times. Compulsions, though they are self-inflicted, arise from various sources, which we explore in this book. There are no simple answers, but the rewards of overcoming a painful behavior are great.

You may wonder about other compulsive behaviors. You are familiar, of course, with your own. There are many subtle as well as obvious forms of compulsion. Let's look at some.

THE SUPERSTUDENT

From the time Jerry was in second grade he had a need to get all As. He sat up straight and listened to his teacher, afraid to miss a word. His work was neat and correct, his oral answers clear and easy to understand.

In third grade, he received a C in art. He was so upset he refused to go home and hid in a neighbor's yard. His mother became worried as time passed and Jerry had not come home. She called the school and was told that Jerry had left with the other children.

As dusk approached, Jerry's mother and the neighbors began to search. Soon his mother spotted her son in his white T-shirt in some shubbery. She picked him up and tried to dry his tears.

"Mom," Jerry cried, "I'm sorry. I did something bad."

"You can tell me," his mother soothed him, "you're a good boy and so smart; you couldn't have done anything horrible."

Jerry began to howl in earnest. His mother always told him how smart he was, and now he had disappointed her. His mother took his hand and led him home. Once there, he handed her his report card—all As except the C in art.

His mother burst out laughing, "you have a C in art! What does that matter! Your excellent academic grades are all that count."

Jerry couldn't believe her. He, the smartest boy his mother had ever known, should have done better. He vowed to himself never to disappoint her again.

By the time Jerry was in high school, he had won every academic award. If a term paper was assigned, he wrote, edited, and rewrote it until it looked like a college graduate's work. He didn't let a comma slip by, or a decimal point be misplaced. He took private art classes, and if a finished picture didn't please him, he'd throw it away and start over.

Jerry worked constantly. He had frequent headaches as he pushed himself on and on. He had a few friends but no time to do anything except study with them.

Jerry longed for free time, to laugh like the other students, to take part in extracurricular activities, but his compulsion to become *the* top student drove him relentlessly on. He wanted to stop, but didn't know how.

Jerry's compulsive behavior clearly shows he had lost control. His self-imposed order to study had to be obeyed by his own dictating self.

- When do you think Jerry's compulsion started? Do you think his mother's constant praise of his intelligence was translated in his mind to, "I must perform well in school"?
- Do you think his special art classes were the result of not believing his mother when she said art wasn't important? Or was his compulsion so great, and his insecurity so overpowering, that he *had* to become a fairly good artist?

Of course, one event, such as Jerry's C on a third-grade report card, was not enough to fuel his obsessive-compulsive behavior for years. A more likely explanation is that Jerry used his incessant studying as a means to nurture himself, as a way not to be hurt. How could anyone criticize a boy who worked as he did? And so he pitted himself against himself. In this way, too, he could avoid intimate relationships with family or friends because he was constantly "busy."

Compulsive behavior is also a way of shutting out pain and anger. When the danger of anything "bad" approaches, a person retreats to behavior that makes him feel in control. Instead of facing problems head-on, the compulsive person goes to great lengths and expends enormous amounts of energy to find a false sense of balance.

SHOP TILL YOU DROP

You have probably seen buttons bearing the slogan, "Shop Till You Drop."

Mary was proud to wear the big red button that identified her to her peers as a "real" shopper.

There was more to it, however. Mary felt "normal" when she wore the slogan. "After all," she reasoned to herself, "I'm not so different from the other girls in school. We all like to go to the mall and spend our money."

But there *was* a difference.

Mary often felt lonely or isolated. Whenever she was depressed, she went shopping, and it instantly changed her mood. Shopping created the illusion that she was no longer lonely. As soon as she entered a store and bought something, she didn't feel alone.

Mary craved emotional connection to others and was afraid of being alone. When she shopped, she felt surrounded by caring people.

She seldom shopped with friends, knowing her compulsion to buy would be noticed. So even though she felt alone, she still preferred going to the mall on her own.

More often than not, Mary returned the items she bought. She didn't really want or need them.

Mary's shopping sprees followed a distinct pattern.

- She was upset and lonely.
- She shopped.
- Her mood lifted.
- She felt guilty about spending so much money.
- She became upset.
- She shopped.
- Her mood lifted.

Mary acted out her feelings through compulsive behavior. Acting out causes an emotional shift, and that is what people like Mary seek. Through acting out, Mary achieved the illusion of being in control. At times, however, as you can see in her pattern, she became upset and created feelings of self-disgust and guilt at her constant need to be in the mall.

* * *

Compulsive behavior is unthinking behavior. People use it to numb themselves and to shield themselves from unpleasant thoughts.

In a way, compulsive behavior is like leaving your self. You do not want to become aware because awareness would make you *face* your discomfort.

To cope with your problem you must realize the difference between compulsive behavior (or the absence of *self*) and awareness, the presence of *self*. It is this difference that changes the entire picture. When you observe what you are doing, you do not behave in the same way as when you are not aware.

Awareness works at a deep level of consciousness. For instance, if you want to go on a shopping spree, but you are aware of the mindlessness of the activity, you have already brought yourself back.

Suppose you're aware that your shopping spree is needless and even tell yourself, "I'm disgusting and selfish . . ." but you decide to go to the mall anyway. Being aware may still change your attitude, at least partly. You know what you are doing. Notice what it feels like to know, to be aware. Is your shopping really the pleasure you hoped it would be?

Awareness is the part of you that wants to change, to grow and to learn. At first, you'll make mistakes, but if you're strong enough to see your actions as mistakes, you can pick yourself up and start again. No one expects you to overcome compulsive behavior overnight.

CONSTANT TALKING

Mark couldn't understand it. Whenever he joined a group at school, it was sure to break up soon afterward.

"They're jerks," he told himself angrily, "they want to do all the talking and leave me out."

The truth could not have been more different. Whenever Mark sidled up to a group, he didn't care who was talking or what the subject was. He had a compulsion to interrupt, to focus all attention on himself.

Generally, Mark talked about the unfairness of things that happened to him. He never seemed to take a breath but went from topic to topic, not noticing the boredom of his fellows. Mark talked in exquisite detail about each instance. When he discussed a teacher's unfairness, he described what the teacher wore and specified the pages in the history book he had been assigned. He elaborated on the temperature in the classroom, the initials carved on his desk by another student, and his nausea whenever he was in class.

No one could interrupt him. He simply didn't hear the other guys. Some of them laughed nervously, others furtively left the group while Mark droned on and on, until he stood alone in the hallway.

"Oh, well," he'd think, "I'll go home. My family *has* to listen to me."

He had no idea when he opened the front door that his mother would take a deep breath, casting about for some way to stop the torrent of words sure to come her way.

Mark had many unresolved feelings and acted them out in an unacceptable social way.

His compulsion to talk pushed the world away and left him alone. Of course, he didn't want to be alone, but his need to cover his true feelings with chatter was greater than his need to conform and to confront issues that bothered him.

Mark also went into fits of rage when he realized no one cared to listen to his negative stories about school.

His anger piled up to such an extent that it often became uncontrollable. Actually, this rage built into anxiety. Sometimes it lasted for moments, at other times for days. Experiencing this anxiety, Mark felt like the whole world was against him and no one liked him. In this state of anxiety,* Mark spoke even more rapidly and his stories lengthened. He talked on and on in a flat voice in the grip of his compulsive behavior.

Incessant talking is a compulsive behavior meant to remove discomfort. The sad part is you cannot remove yourself from discomfort without removing yourself from a large part of life.

A frightening aspect of having to talk on and on is that it gives one a sense of being almost possessed. It seems impossible to be quiet and to listen.

The possession is sadly of one's own making. It takes control of one and pushes away the sense that other people exist.

The compulsive talker continues on and on, to the dismay of those unfortunate enough to be near him.

RIGID SCHEDULES

Lorie, a tenth-grader, was so pretty that other students were sure she'd be a star or model some day. Her long, blonde hair cascaded in perfect waves down her back. Her stylish clothes matched her shoes and bag. Her big, blue eyes fringed with long, dark lashes completed a picture of near perfection.

Despite her attributes, however, quite a few students felt uncomfortable around Lorie. She seldom smiled as she hurried across the yard or through hallways to classes.

During lectures, she held herself rigidly, her back straight, hand clutching her pen as she took notes.

Lorie often peered furtively at her watch and double-checked the time with the classroom clock. Time seemed very important to her.

When she took tests, her face was pinched as she hurried to finish before time was up. She was never late for class, never came home late from school, and always needed to know the family plans for the whole week.

One day John, the class president, asked her to go to a movie on Friday night.

"I'd like to go," she said, "but I help my mother shop on Fridays."

"Wouldn't she understand just once?" John wondered.

"Oh, I'm sure she'd give in, but shopping on Fridays is our schedule. I don't think it's fair to break a schedule."

"O.K., O.K.," John said rather impatiently. "How about Saturday night?"

"That's fine. I have nothing planned," Lorie answered.

On Saturday morning, however, John felt sick. He had a fever and a sore throat. He called Lorie to explain that the date was off.

"May I have a rain check?" he asked.

"We had a date—a schedule to keep," Lorie said unsympathetically. "I'm sure if you'd rest all day, you'd be fine by tonight. But since our time together doesn't mean anything to you, I don't want to see you again."

John was shocked. Time? Schedules? What did Lorie mean? What about his illness?

Meanwhile, Lorie spent the weekend adhering to her schedule: two hours of piano practice, one hour cleaning and rearranging her closet, two hours in conversation with her parents, and so on. She always diligently observed the amount of time allotted to each activity.

*　　*　　*

Lorie's compulsion with time was used as a safety net for her emotions. As long as she stuck to a rigid schedule, nothing unpleasant or hurtful could interfere. Such thoughts swirled around her mind as she tried to shut out life with the tension under which she put herself.

She may have seemed self-centered, but in fact she was centered on her compulsive schedules at a cost to *herself*. Lorie felt little trust, and since trust creates safety, Lorie had none. Her rigid schedule gave her the fantasy of being safe.

Imagine an argument Lorie must often have had with herself:

"Should I stick to my schedules, or should I go out with other kids?"

"It's okay to stick to my schedules."

"It's not okay to stick to my schedules."

"I'll get in trouble."

"I don't care if I get in trouble and nobody likes me."

In this type of conversation, the self tries to control the compulsive person. It is torture to live that way. Lorie's compulsion held her in a viselike grip.

- How do you think she might have helped herself?
- Do you think it's possible to change rigid compulsive behavior? How?

STUCK IN THE HOUSE

Joanne graduated from high school in June, which her teachers, parents, and friends considered a miracle. Joanne had the longest list of absenteeism in the school. She simply couldn't leave home and was terrified of the outside world.

Her parents had tried to get her to see a counselor, but since it would have meant leaving the house, she had refused to go. The school had sent experts to find out why Joanne refused to attend classes, but she couldn't answer their questions.

Finally, a home tutor had been assigned to help Joanne get her diploma. To her amazement, she had found Joanne to be an excellent student, interested in many subjects. However, when the tutor had suggested that they go out to lunch or to a museum, Joanne had steadfastly refused.

When she received her diploma, Joanne did not attend the graduation. The prom, of course, was out of the questions. Her parents were very unhappy about Joanne, but they didn't know how to help her.

Two months after graduation, Joanne came down with pneumonia. An ambulance took her to the hospital, screaming and coughing and gasping for air.

In the hospital, a doctor discovered Joanne's problem: agoraphobia. The word is Greek for "fear of the market-place." In Joanne's case, it was fear of the outside world. She stayed in her house, a virtual prisoner of compulsive behavior.

You can see that Joanne's behavior was self-defeating and even disabling. In her life story, there must have been an incident of emotional hurt. Her compulsion was a clue, but Joanne, like many agoraphobics, had no idea she was engaging in compulsive behavior.

Joanne was not yet ready to take steps to unravel her story, nor was she able to confront the problems that had led to her agoraphobia.

Some people remain in their houses all their lives. They could be helped. If they were willing to follow the trail of clues leading to their self-imprisonment, they could eventually become free.

"FAT DEBBIE"

Debbie, fourteen and with a beautiful figure, had many arguments with her single mother.

Her mother was working on her doctor's degree in psychology and often used Debbie as her "patient."

"Debbie," she'd say, "you're fourteen now. Do you have sexual feelings yet?" Then she'd sit with pencil poised to take notes on Debbie's expected reply.

Debbie usually ran out of the house without answering, her face burning with shame and anger. "How can Mom humiliate me like this?" she'd think. "I must be different from my sisters. Mother takes everything out on me."

Debbie looked at herself in the mirror often and hated all the signs of her body's change into womanhood.

"I'm fat," she decided one day—and virtually stopped eating.

Debbie became anorexic and after six months weighed a mere 79 pounds. While she starved herself compulsively, she felt powerful. Her mother worried, her sisters paid attention to her, and best of all, Debbie thought, her body had reverted to that of a child. Her breasts were gone, she no longer had her monthly period, and her body hair was disappearing.

Debbie fantasized having power, but in a deeper way she felt herself unable to meet her own needs or solve her problems with her outrageous mother. Even if she tried, she thought, she would not get what she needed. Underneath her fantasy, Debbie felt completely helpless. That's why the illusion of power offered by anorexia was so irresistible to Debbie. It was a dangerous trade-off. She also tried bingeing and purging, called bulimia. She would stuff herself—twelve doughnuts, an entire chicken, and a bag of potato chips at a sitting—and then make herself vomit to remain at her "ideal" 79 pounds.

Finally, Debbie was taken to a hospital, where she hovered between life and death.

The story has a happy ending. Debbie's father finally stepped in, and she went to live with him. She went to a psychiatrist and overcame her eating disorders. It was hard work, but Debbie did it.

Her mother? Her mother received a doctor's degree and opened a practice in eating disorders!

Debbie had been used all the way.

GAMBLING

One of the compulsions currently reaching epidemic proportions in high schools is gambling. It involves millions of teens and appears to be uncontrollable.

What is the appeal of gambling? Legalized games of chance bring in well over $200 billion a year in the United States, starting with state lotteries and continuing through horse racing, sports betting, and casinos. With all that money at stake, a giant industry run by sophisticated businessmen has arisen. They study every aspect of the gambler's psychology to design the most enticing games.

For example, most forms of gambling pay out 92 percent of the money they take in. Over the long haul, however, players win a little every so often—just enough to keep them interested. Psychologists know that intermittent rewards are addictive.

In Los Angeles, Channel 2 Action News (an affiliate of CBS) reported in February 1993 the seriousness of gambling compulsions among teens.

"They play as hard as the big boys," reporter Harvey Levin told the TV audience.

The biggest interest is sports gambling. In schools all over the country, thousands of dollars were bet on the Super Bowl. Bookies were easy to find, according to undercover agents at Beverly Hills High School.

One student, Jonathan, explained that he *had* to gamble. Not only did he bet on sports, but he went to the casinos in Las Vegas twice weekly. At his school, in Calabasas, he bet as much as $400 a game. He is so compulsive about it that he has stolen money and rings from his mother to pay for his habit.

Other teens go to chariot horse racing. How do they get in? At Los Alamitos Race Track in California, no questions were asked as the teens placed their wagers. When the reporter asked officials why they admitted minors, the reply implied that they couldn't tell the ages. They also promised to get greater security in the future.

Dured Jacobs, a nationally recognized expert, says that gambling is becoming an enormous problem among teens. One in every ten has a gambling habit. How is such a compulsion spotted?

1. The teen plays games even if the outcome is never in doubt.
2. The teen may watch games on multiple TV sets simultaneously.

3. The teen collects old ticket stubs.

Where do these teens get the money for their addictive behavior?

Many have jobs, but others have learned to manipulate their parents by lying about why they need money. If nothing else works, compulsive gamblers simply steal or go into debt.

A gambling compulsions starts to flourish at the point of panic. At first, it may seem like fun if winning occurs more often than losing.

However, as the teen begins to lose, real fear sets in. "I'll make it up next time," is the promise, but the next time may be another loss. Ongoing tension ensues between the gambler's normal self and his compulsive self, and it becomes more and more compelling. The person's values, priorities, and loved ones are attacked through constant borrowing, stealing, and manipulation.

Now the gambler may have a secondary compulsion: borrowing and getting deeper and deeper into debt as losses grow. The two compulsions begin to reinforce each other.

Depression is bound to follow, and often a kind of paranoia sets in. The teen who thought gambling was just for fun is now alienated from himself and others as he looks for the big win.

A gruesome case of teen gambling happened in a high school where students bet $200 on whether or not their teacher could be killed. Fortunately, undercover police discovered the bet and the teacher survived.

Imagine, however, what it would have been like had the teacher died. All their lives the students would have felt part of a murder.

Compulsive gambling makes a person feel empty after a

while, whether he wins or loses. He wrestles every day with the anxiety that he will be found out.

Compulsive gambling does not develop in a vacuum. It usually begins in a family in which needs are not met. In such surroundings many types of compulsion can arise—overreacting, shopping, drinking—and gambling. Each compulsion may express itself differently, but they share a common system of denial: Promises to stop are made but are impossible to keep.

In such cases, *each* member of the family needs to take responsibility—not by blaming others, but by looking inside himself or herself.

If gambling is popular in your school, take stock of what it has done to you if you are a participant.

1. Are you dependent on others to keep your compulsion going?
2. Do you have enough money of your own?
3. Are you in debt with no idea how to pay back?
4. Does winning give you a false sense of control?
5. Does losing make you want to gamble more frequently?
6. Do you trust others?
7. Are you afraid of being rejected by your peers if you stop gambling?
8. Do you think about the next bet all the time?
9. Do you tell yourself, "I can handle it" but have fearful times when you realize you can't?

If you are uncomfortable answering these questions, you must think about getting help and allow yourself to breathe freely once again.

Gambling and being in debt go hand in hand. Gambling and manipulating your parents go hand in hand. Finally, at the most desperate stage, gambling and stealing go hand in hand.

To cope with your problem, you must examine the tight web in which you find yourself and get help to escape it. To get information:

In New Jersey, call   In South Dakota, call:
(609) 347-0800   Hotline 1-800-529-0043
(609) 599-9383   (605) 229-0760

In California, call: In Ontario, Canada, call:
(916) 323-0202   (416) 499-9800

In the U.S. you can also call Gambler's Anonymous (see phonebook).

COMPULSIVE DEBTORS

Going into debt has been described as the "American way—everybody owes everybody." It's not surprising that today's teens, with their jobs, cars, bank accounts, and nearly adult life-styles, get into debt almost as often as their parents do.

Debt means borrowing money from a bank, on a credit card, or from some other source to purchase something you can't afford. You pay back the debt over time, with interest. Lenders are supposed to make loans only to people who are responsible and can pay them back on time. But with so many banks and corporations competing for the profitable lending business, sometimes caution goes out the window.

Even a dog can get a credit card these days. A credit card company accidentally gets the name of somebody's pet—let's say Jane Smith's cat, Jinx. Understandably curious, Jane Smith opens the letter to her cat and reads: "Congratulations, Mr. J. Smith. Because of your outstanding credit record, you have been preapproved for a credit card with a borrowing limit of $3,000. Just fill in the application and we'll send you the card."

Just for fun, Jane Smith fills in the application and mails it back. A few weeks later, a shiny new credit card arrives in the mail. On it is embossed the name "Jinx Smith." Thank to computers, Jane's cat now owns his very own credit card.

Teenagers sometimes get credit cards in much the same way. More often, a parent cosigns the application, agreeing to be responsible if the teen does not make the payments. Either way, after a teen establishes a good payment record with one card, other lending institutions decide he or she is a good credit risk. Offers for more cards quickly follow.

It's a normal part of American society to borrow amounts that you can afford to pay back. But debt can become a problem in two ways. First, you may have so many cards and owe so much money that all the little monthly payments add up to a monthly total bigger than you can pay.

Second, even if you can keep up with small monthly payments, the balance can grow insidiously because of the interest, the amount the bank charges to lend you money in the first place. Loans can come with a 21 percent rate of interest, which is compounded monthly. That means if you don't pay off the whole loan fast, you wind up owing a lot more than you bargained for at the end of the year.

Where does compulsion enter in? Like compulsive shoppers, compulsive debtors feel that they must spend whatever they can. They spend to the limit on each card— not because they need the items purchased, but because they can't help themselves. If the money (credit) is there, they *must* spend it. This type of person also feels compelled to accept every credit card offered. It is not unusual for a compulsive debtor to owe money to more than a dozen different lenders. Credit cards can come from banks, stores, and even automobile manufacturers.

In this case, however, the compulsive person is spending borrowed money—and the consequences can quickly spiral out of control.

Debt compulsion can arise from many sources. Like all compulsions, it is an unhealthy way to find short-term emotional release. What sets the compulsive debtor apart from other compulsive people? Often it is a problem with self-esteem.

The compulsive debtor may not have lived up to his own or others' expectations in some important area of life. He or she needs positive reinforcement. Each new credit card is like a badge of honor saying, "You're all right. We trust you enough to give you this tool and lend you thousands of dollars."

Each new purchase becomes a "test," which shows the compulsive person that the lending company really does trust and value him or her as a customer. Running the cards up to their maximum and keeping them there is like getting continuous, maximum levels of trust and approval. Like many other compulsions, the real agenda behind the repeated behavior has little to do with the activity itself— in this case, borrowing and buying. Instead, it is repeatedly used to bolster the person's weak self-esteem.

HOW CAN ONE DEFINE COMPULSION?

A compulsion is behavior that is repeated over and over again, to change a mood, to alter a bad feeling to a good one. Compulsions cover up sad feelings and an inner emptiness.

A behavior becomes compulsive in the way it is used— when it is driven, consistent, and done over and over again. We have seen several compulsions. Actually, any behavior can fall into that category—incessant exercise, flirting, eating ice cream, speeding on freeways, having to have every hair in place, and many more.

Compulsive behavior is the enemy of self-esteem. It can be overcome and completely eliminated. It can be replaced by positive feelings. The pressure lifts, and freedom and relaxation become the reality.

CHAPTER 2

Who Is Likely to Be Compulsive?

Perhaps you have compulsions because you don't feel safe in the world. You have a strong sense of uncertainty. You need positive people around you to give you some relief from the feeling that your life is like a house of cards about to collapse.

How often a behavior is repeated is directly related to how much you are out of touch with your real feelings. These feelings are hidden because they are so painful that you don't allow them to come to consciousness. The idea then is to shop excessively, or telephone, or work constantly, or any number of activities that do not involve you emotionally but create the fantasy of control. This fantasy finally becomes your enemy.

FAMILY PATTERNS

All too often parents of kids with compulsions have an ideal of the "perfect child." During the child's growing years they push these unrealistic expectations onto him or her.

Such parents are full of self-doubt. They see everything in terms of black and white, right and wrong, good and bad. Their children often feel like failures. Such a situation easily begins a compulsion toward perfection.

To Be the Best

Helen grew up in a family where the rules were firm. Seldom were change or flexibility considered.

Helen was told that if she wanted to go to college, she'd have to earn a scholarship, and As were the only acceptable grades. Helen's mother stressed the fact that Dad didn't make enough money to send her to a really good university. As a result, Helen came to consider both her father and herself failures.

Strangely enough, Helen's father always praised her. He thought her achievements were wonderful. He often brought her little presents to show how proud he was of her. But her father's approval and the presents never made up for her feeling that to her mother Helen was a failure. She just was never perfect enough. How could she be?

The pressure of her mother's impossible standards hooked Helen on performance in school. She studied incessantly. She lost her natural joy of learning and pressured herself to become her mother's perfect little darling, an all-A student.

As the pressure built up, it clearly needed an outlet. This outlet was compulsive behavior, a kind of addiction to perfection, not only in school, but in all areas of her life. Helen began to have great expectations not only of herself but of her friends. When they disappointed her by canceling a date or seeing a movie she didn't approve of, she felt betrayed, angry, and bitter. She made her friends bigger than life. When they didn't live up to her expectations, she dropped them.

The Greeks have a word for this: hubris, having too much pride. This was Helen's downfall. She had created an idealized self, a perfect self, and no one in her world was allowed to make a mistake. The other side of Helen's emotional makeup was low self-esteem from being unable to live up to her mother's impossible expectations, and later her own.

Helen's compulsive perfectionism is clear and tragic.

- Could Helen have turned to her father for help when she was younger?
- How did Helen's fear of her mother turn her behavior into a copy of her mother's?

LOSS OF A PARENT

Another source of compulsive behavior can be the early loss of a mother or father.

When young children lose a parent to death, they feel many emotions besides sadness. Children often feel responsible for their parent's death, and they feel guilty.

Suppose a boy doesn't get his way with his mother and becomes very angry with her. He slams the door to his room, mumbling to himself, "I wish she was dead." A few months later a sudden short illness ends the mother's life, and the boy's guilt becomes unbearable.

Another way a child's feelings come out at the death of a parent is in the form of anger at being left. But he can't show this anger, so it is turned inward. When that happens, self-hatred and feelings of worthlessness grow. The child feels powerless and frightened.

Such a child may turn to compulsive behavior. He may

say to himself, "People can hurt me, but material things can't." He may become an avid stamp collector to the exclusion of other activities. As he grows into his teens, the important people pictured on the stamps become his heroes and heroines. Their value to him lies in their fame and their emotional distance. As he trades the stamps, he associates himself with the well-known faces, as though they were people he knew. This gives him a false sense of self-esteem. His compulsive buying and selling of stamps can be a way of dealing with the anger and hurt over the loss of his mother. He no longer has to deal with the feelings of a family member. He is on his way to an adult compulsion that masquerades as a hobby but is really an outlet for his anger, sorrow, and insecurity.

A FAMILY IN CONFLICT

All too many families need to work very hard to make ends meet. This was the case with Jane's parents. Both worked and came home dead tired every night.

Usually, Jane and her mother cooked dinner while her dad watched the news on TV. At the table, he ate in silence. When his wife would ask mildly, "How did you like the steak?" he'd mumble something.

Jane might tell her dad, "I helped Mom with dinner. Wasn't the dessert scrumptious?"

Her father invariably became angry. "Who told you to help her? All you want is praise, praise, praise. Big deal." He'd storm out of the dining room to continue watching TV until midnight.

Jane's mother was always upset by this. When her daughter went to her room to do her homework, she often took her special treats to make up for her father's coldness.

Sometimes Jane and her mother went to the mall, and

Jane was allowed to buy lots of clothes on condition that she hide them and not tell her father. He was not interested in her and became the family "enemy."

By the time Jane was seventeen, she had a part-time job and spent more than she earned on clothes. She shopped every spare moment she had. She owed money to various stores and had no idea how to pay them. Often she returned her purchases.

Her father's refusal to communicate in a positive way, and her mother's secret indulgence helped to lead Jane to compulsive shopping.

Many compulsive spenders have no idea what they want or what they need. They frequently have no goals in life. If they do, they often feel sure they can't achieve them and so refuse to try. They feel helpless when confronted with stress or frustration, and their compulsive spending gives them a temporary sensation of being in control.

In Jane's case, her father's anger and her mother's indulgence made her feel lonely. She couldn't really turn to either parent. "Where do I fit in?" she wondered. It seemed her parents were on a collision course, each trying to hurt the other. "Is this what life is all about?" she'd question. Trying to cope without a support system is difficult at best. At worst, it can lead to despair—and an effort to escape through compulsive behavior.

ATTITUDES THAT BREED COMPULSIONS

Sometimes a child notices something new to him and asks the parents about it. Perhaps it's a bra, or a bottle of medicine, or a breathing device for an asthmatic.

If the parent answers, "Oh, it's nothing," the child may think his observation had no value.

Later, however, as the child becomes a teenager he *knows* that his mother and sister wear bras, he *knows* his asthmatic brother uses a breathing device—and he also realizes that his parents can't accept these realities of life, brushing them away as "nothings." The message is: "In our family, these matters are not discussed and in fact need not exist at all." He begins to wonder what else exists that is not in the family script. He may even begin to doubt his own observation. Maybe his brother just had frequent colds but not asthma—maybe his mother and sister don't wear bras. He can begin to reject the reality of his senses and follow the family pattern of denial.

After a while, however, he will pay a price for following the family's perceptions. His own perceptions become weaker and weaker. Is he following his reality, or letting it go in favor of his family's reality? This situation causes confusion, and the boy probably no longer knows if he has a mind of his own.

If you think you are caught in this kind of trap, think about these questions:

- Does my family withhold information from me that might threaten the image of the "perfect" family?
- Does my family refuse to recognize my feelings and try to change them to conform to our "ideal" picture?
- Does my family keep me stuck in childhood by reminding me what a compliant little one I was and expecting me to behave the same way as a teenager?

If you answer "yes," be aware that compulsive behavior could be triggered by the sense of unreality in your family structure. When the level of insecurity rises, compulsions often seem to offer safety. Of course, you know that compulsive behavior cannot make you truly safe or secure, but it can seem a measure of defense against a world that is too hard to bear.

Compulsion is self-defeating, and on some level the compulsive person knows it. But confronting the problem is very hard. What's going on inside hurts too much. The compulsive distances himself from painful reality rather than dealing with it. It's too frightening to face the confusion and pain.

FEARS

Miriam was brought up in Germany during the Holocaust. Every day brought a new horror.

Her father fled to America, hoping to have the rest of the family join him. Her grandparents were taken to a concentration camp and gassed to death. She herself had an eye condition that might lead to blindness.

On and on the torment went, until she and her mother finally were able to rejoin her father in Pennsylvania. But hopeful as her new life was, Miriam carried a constant burden of guilt about those she'd left behind to die.

As time passed, she realized that no one wanted to hear her sad tale over and over again. She repressed her memories of Nazi Germany, learned to smile, became a cheerleader, and went out on dates. She was now a popular girl in high school.

Her parents hoped that she had come out of her depression, but she often cried at night in her room. She wanted to find a way to make the world a better place.

Miriam was a good student, and she stayed late at school to tutor students who needed help. Then she rushed home to help out because both of her parents worked. While dinner was cooking, she'd vacuum or do the laundry. Homework done, Miriam would greet her parents each night with a big smile. She did not want her parents to suffer even a little bit.

The more Miriam did for others, the greater became her compulsion to help. She joined environmental groups, helped clean up poor neighborhoods, worked to help the homeless. Still it wasn't enough. There wasn't a moment in her day that wasn't filled. The smile remained on Miriam's face, and her compulsive helping kept her from thinking. Only at night did the tears come, and often she didn't know why. Miriam had put her tragedy in the furthest recesses of her mind.

Let's stop a minute to reflect on the cost of compulsions.

- Does a compulsion cost a price in friendships?
- Can compulsions cost money?
- Can compulsions take away free time?
- Are compulsions harmful emotionally or spiritually?
- Do compulsions leave you tired by sapping your energies?
- Can compulsive behavior hurt your health?
- Can compulsions interfere with your performance at school?

Compulsive behavior *can* exact a price, and it often costs more than you realize.

THE NEED TO BE GOOD ENOUGH

The fear of disapproval, of criticism and rejection makes the compulsive teenager constantly question himself or herself. Something always whispers in your ear, "You're not good enough," "You look ridiculous in those clothes," "Why did you do that?" The worst part is that people say you're "self-conscious," whereas your "self" is the last thing you want to be conscious of.

Maria

Maria's mother was a housekeeper, and her father was a janitor in an office building. They constantly adjured her to "remember her place," not to aspire to college or a profession.

Maria was exceptionally bright. In high school, she particularly liked science. But whenever she was called on, the compulsion whispered in her ear, "Don't answer . . . don't show off. . . remember your place," and the teacher went on to another student. On exams, Maria almost always had a perfect grade. Did this make her happy? No! She blamed herself for getting a better mark than her classmates. On the other hand, she was ashamed because she thought she really did deserve the high grade. Back and forth her thoughts would go, leaving her no peace.

Maria would have given anything to get out of the jail she'd built for herself. Fear of disapproval became the overriding factor in her life. Her put-downs and compulsive monitoring of her behavior prevented her from moving forward, keeping her stuck in fear.

Maria's compulsion not to express herself honestly became her unrealistic safety blanket in avoiding being "more" or "better" than her parents.

MEETING NEEDS

As you can see, many compulsive behaviors are really ways of feeling safe by not facing a problem. What can you do to cope with problems you don't want to look at?

The first thing is to admit to yourself that you have needs. This doesn't mean you're a "needy" poor little thing. Many people in our society take the attitude that one should not have needs—but even they have needs of their own. These people pontificate that if we don't fuss about our needs, they'll just go away.

Nothing could be further from the truth. Unmet needs grow if ignored and often lead to compulsions.

Your needs change from the time you are born until the time you die. As a baby your needs may seem simple: food, clothing, a warm blanket. But the most important need of all is love. With love during the first year of life, you learn to trust.

If, however, you felt insecure and never knew what was coming next, compulsions may have rushed in to fill the emptiness. The feeling of helplessness, of not having power is the beginning of compulsive behavior.

If you failed to get what you needed as a tiny baby, you may still have times of feeling like a very young child.

You must come to realize that to meet your needs you may have to *take* the power to meet them—or have them met by others outside your family.

If you can consciously step aside and look at what was in the past and what is now, you can begin to take the power you need to break your compulsion and take responsibility for yourself.

As you meet your needs, you will have less reason to go through the endless cycle of compulsive behavior. Your self-esteem will rise in direct proportion to your abandonment of the rituals of compulsion.

As you learn to care for yourself, you'll be amazed at how well you can care for others. People will sense your growing inner strength as you live in reality and throw off the shackles of compulsive behavior.

By the time you're a teenager, you meet many of your own needs, but you still need encouragement, positive feedback from your family, approval, and love. The one need that never changes is love.

As a teenager, however, you also have a need to become more independent. If your parents keep you on too tight a rein, it is likely that compulsions will look good to you.

Kenny

Kenny was an average student in his junior year in high school. He had a pleasant personality and was often asked by friends to go to football games or dances. Whenever he asked to use the car, his parents would answer, "Well, it's probably all right, but you have to mow the lawn, clean your room, and have all your homework done."

Kenny would work furiously to get everything done. Then, showered, dressed, he would to ask his father for the keys to the car.

His mother often would stop him.

"Kenny," she'd say slowly in the maddening tone that Kenny hated, "you forgot to edge the lawn."

His father, keys in hand, would put them back in his pocket.

"Sorry, son," he'd say, shaking his head, "but you didn't finish the job. I'm afraid you'll have to call your friends and tell them you can't go."

Kenny would argue. "But can't I edge the lawn tomorrow? I did everything else . . ." His mother would interrupt him, "Sorry dear, a half-done job isn't good enough. Maybe you can go out next week."

Kenny was left feeling worthless, powerless, frustrated, and furious.

Running out, he would edge the lawn and rake the gravel. Next, he'd weed and water the flower beds, then reclean his room. He'd wax the floor, take his books and stereo from the shelves and dust under everything. "I'll show them," he'd mumble, feeling a temporary sense of power. "They'll be sorry."

Meanwhile his parents sat downstairs, feeling smug and content. They had controlled their son.

Kenny's compulsive cleaning finally became a daily ritual that gave him a false sense of power. He thought he was punishing his parents. Neither they nor he were *aware* that Kenny was sublimating his anger and frustration with compulsion.

"I'll show them," he thought.

"He learned a lesson," the parents thought.

The very first step in coping with compulsion is to be *aware*.

- What are you doing?
- Why are you doing it?
- How do you feel when you are engaged in your compulsive behavior?
- Does it work?
- Is your mood changed during your ritual of compulsive behavior?

Be aware of the reason for your compulsive behavior. Monitor yourself. Notice *when* you begin to do things you *have* to do.

Kenny's compulsion started when his parents frustrated him beyond belief. It continued because he felt powerless and angry. As soon as he saw his room after school, his anger overwhelmed him and he started to clean. This let him avoid facing the fact that he felt his parents were unfair or even that he didn't love them.

If Kenny had been more aware of his powerful emotions of anger and fear, the compulsion might have lifted and let the real feelings show through. He might have observed himself and his cycle of compulsion, recognized his unmet needs, and moved to the beginning stage of dealing with his destructive behavior.

Kenny's family could be considered dysfunctional. They don't work well together, and they react in negative, hurtful ways toward one another. In such a family, the members often need a fantasy to keep them from feeling constant pain—and that fantasy is often compulsive behavior.

Remember Kenny's mother had a slow, deliberate way of speaking. Perhaps she, too, felt more in control by pretending she was never angry. She, too, was in a state of denial, dishonest about her feelings, acting out her fantasy as the calm parent.

Kenny could change his fantasy by becoming conscious of it. It can be broken if he looks honestly at his role in the family, recognizes his anger, and confronts his feelings. He will need support from counselors, friends, and even his parents to break free of his compulsive behavior.

FEAR OF PUNISHMENT

Robin's Mother

Robin and her mother just couldn't get along. Neighbors heard their fights, waitresses in restaurants pretended they didn't notice the vicious arguments between mother and daughter, and Louis, father and husband, turned a deaf ear to the constant shouting. Worst of all, their arguments were about trifles such as the color of a dress, or a movie one liked and the other didn't.

Robin felt completely unloved by her parents. "Obviously," she thought, "my mother shows me at every turn that my opinion doesn't count, and my father doesn't want to get involved."

One day there was relative quiet in the house. Robin was studying for finals, and her mother sat with a newspaper. Every so often, Robin looked up and noticed her mother's lips moving.

"Mother, what's going on? You're not reading out loud, are you?" she asked sarcastically.

Fear crossed her mother's face. "No, no I'm not," and she burst into tears.

Robin's surprise turned to sudden compassion. "What's wrong, Mother?" she asked. The older woman revealed a long-held secret.

"When I was a little girl my parents constantly punished me. They'd accuse me of stealing, of annoying them by reading aloud, or being sneaky, and they'd spank me. Today, I guess it's called child abuse."

Robin sat close to her mother for the first time in years and put her arm across the shaking shoulders.

"I tried to tune out their accusations by counting things. When I counted, I couldn't hear them. I knew how many steps were in everybody's house, how many buttons were on my father's shirts, how many cracks were in the sidewalk in front of my school. Just now I was counting the words in the newspaper."

"But you're grown up now," Robin soothed, "are you still afraid?"

"I guess I never thought about it before," her mother answered.

"Why do we fight so much?" Robin wondered suddenly.

"You interrupt my counting things when you talk to me," was the incredible answer, "and I get very nervous and have to start counting all over again. I'm so sorry; I've made your life miserable, haven't I?" she sniffled.

"I didn't have to argue about everything either," Robin admitted. "I just thought you didn't love me."

Her mother cried hysterically for quite a while. Between sobs, she admitted that Robin's father seldom talked because he knew better than to interrupt her counting compulsion. He'd given up years ago.

Robin still wondered about one thing: If her mother knew the reason for her counting, why couldn't she stop?

Robin's mother had never gotten over being the abused child. Her past had shaped her and cast her in the role of the unwanted, abused misfit.

When she grew up and had a baby, she was delighted— until her little girl began to talk. All the old fears returned, and unconsciously she gave Robin the power to punish her by allowing the child to fight with her. That enabled her to feel like a victim again, pursuing her compulsion of counting. Only then could she shut out the world and gain a false sense of safety.

Despite Robin's longing for love, when her mother broke down she felt the older woman's desperate need. As her mother confided in her, Robin likened the problem to being under a spell. She determined to help her mother break the spell and become the adult she could have been all along.

Robin had a long talk with her father, and they found a therapist to help her mother. Robin no longer felt the need to argue in a bid for attention. She began to receive love and admiration from both her parents as she helped her mother. Sometimes she felt there had been a role reversal, that she, Robin, had become the mother. But she was confident that as her parent improved they would end up very good friends.

FEAR OF FACING YOURSELF

One of the biggest tragedies is the teenager who thinks he's just not enough. Enough for whom? Enough for what?

Of course, this thought is not verbalized. It is expressed through rejection of everything about himself. He may tell himself:

"I'm ugly."

"I'm stupid."

"I'm clumsy—no wonder no one wants me on their team."

"I'm no good."

"I'm a nerd."

When you have such thoughts, you weigh everything that happens to you on the scale of your mistaken belief. Then you express it through your behavior.

Marigold's Prize

Marigold's school gave awards at the end of the year: for the most helpful boy or girl, the best speaker, the best athlete, and the top prize, for *highest grade point average*.

When the assembly began, everyone buzzed about who

would win in the various categories. Marigold slid down in her seat and "knew" deep inside that she'd wouldn't win anything. It had nothing to do with the teachers' committee that made the choices. Marigold never even tried to compete. She just "knew" she wasn't "enough."

The program began, and the students quieted down. As each winner was announced and went to the stage to receive a trophy, loud applause followed.

Suddenly, Marigold heard her name. She looked around to see if anyone else was named Marigold, but no one stood up. Slowly, she rose to her feet and in a trance walked down the aisle and to the stage. Marigold had won the major award of the year, the academic award for achievement. The trophy seemed almost as big as she was, and as she heard the thunderous applause she was sure a mistake had been made.

Marigold had a false sense of self and could not believe in herself even when she held the proof of her achievement in her hands. She felt she was living a lie and couldn't wait to go home.

Once there, she hid the trophy in the back of her closet. Locking her door, she got out large sheets of construction paper, scissors, and a big plastic bag. She set out to cut the paper into tiny pieces until the bag was filled with confetti. While she snipped and cut, she didn't think. The activity froze time and put her life on hold so she didn't have to face the problem of "I'm not enough."

When the bag was full of multicolored confetti, Marigold put it in the closet alongside her trophy and ten other bags full of little pieces of cut paper.

Marigold's compulsive behavior created for her a never-never land in which she didn't have to take risks. She never wanted to grow up, since she knew she wasn't "enough." Her compulsion reduced her tension in the unreal world she had created for herself and provided temporary comfort.

Recovery is possible for the compulsive person who thinks he's "not enough." One way to help yourself is to become aware of the beliefs that start your behavior and to reprogram yourself with healthier thoughts. As a compulsive person, you are not functioning at your best. You have to change your feelings about yourself, change your values, and realize you are an important person.

If you think that to be "enough" you have to be absolutely perfect and you then make a mistake, you will have succeeded in feeling like a failure. But you can *change* this belief by beginning to think of yourself as okay just as you are. Mistakes are allowed. Everyone makes them. A mistake does not mean you're not "enough."

What are some healthy ways of thinking about yourself?

- I am enough just as I am.
- Feelings are not bad, but denying they exist is.
- I am not perfect—that's all right.
- I can cope with problems (with support, a little at a time).
- I am the one who has to see my needs are met.
- Compulsive behavior cannot give me real power or make me feel good about myself.

When you decide to cope with your problem and seem to be getting better, don't be surprised if suddenly you backtrack and say, "I knew it, I'm not enough. I deserve nothing." Keep at it! Don't stay stuck. Just be aware that a few days of feeling awful are *part* of your getting better.

You need to consciously think of yourself as worthwhile and accept the good things in your life—improved relationships, self-esteem. Let your compulsions go! Don't use up your energy trying to control everyone's opinion of you. Accept yourself, mistakes and all.

Chris

Chris was six years old when she began to swim in competitions. Tall for her age, she had the ideal body for a swimmer and easily beat other six-year-olds.

Her father began to see the potential in Chris and constantly urged the coach to give her extra hard workouts, which the coach refused. Chris's father began attending all her workouts. If he felt she wasn't doing her best, he'd call her out behind the dressing rooms and whip her mercilessly with his belt.

"Now let's see you really work," he'd say in a quiet threatening manner, "or you won't get dinner."

Chris learned early that swimming was associated with pain and fear.

Chris won medal after medal. Her father bought her extravagant gifts if she won first place. If not, no dinner. Practice increased from one hour to five daily. Meets were scheduled every weekend. Now both her parents told her, "You *will* go to the Olympics."

Chris wondered in her child's mind, "If I don't go to the Olympics, what will happen to me?"

The groundwork for compulsion had been laid. A compulsion sneaks up on you and before you know it dominates your behavior. It becomes almost inseparable from your personality.

Chris's compulsion was that of a driven athlete. She lifted weights in between workouts, refused to eat candy or junk food, and kept her daily times on a chart to see if she was improving. Chris also did well at school, and by the time she was fourteen she had a reputation in swim circles as a wonder child. Her incessant drive, prompted by fear of her father, drove her on and on. She never had a day to relax, and the only time she socialized was with teammates while waiting her turn at swim meets.

Chris went to the Junior Olympics, and everyone was convinced she would make the big Olympics.

Her parents surrounded her, talking strategy, time, whom to watch out for. Swimming, studying, and driving herself became a way of life for Chris. It was hard to tell which was her personality and which was the compulsion. Chris told everyone how much she loved her sport.

The year before trials for the Summer Olympics, Chris met a boy in school. After three months she became pregnant. Her father sent her to a home for unwed mothers and told her never to come home again.

Chris was lucky. The home listened to her story and found a therapist for her.

Chris's compulsion had built up over many years. The level of her fear and insecurity had risen to the danger zone, until she felt safe only while engaged in her compulsive behavior.

While getting professional help, Chris tried to give up her compulsion to work and to study. Of course, she couldn't swim, but her room was the cleanest, her willingness to help was constant. Her compulsiveness actually grew worse at first. It was very difficult to give up. As her true feelings began to come out, she had to face the pain her father had inflicted for so long and the knowledge that her mother had never stood up for her.

Slowly, over the months, Chris was able to find a strong grown-up inside her. She began to treat herself more kindly. She gave in to tiredness, she made friends, she talked about her life to her roommate, to her therapist, and to the housemother.

Chris began to get the compulsion out of her system and to externalize it. There were still moments when anxiety overtook her, but she began to learn that she could live without her compulsion.

After Chris's baby was born, a good foster home was found for the two of them. Chris finished high school and became a nursery school teacher. She never played competitive games with her young charges; she just allowed them to be themselves.

THE NEED TO PUNISH YOURSELF

Often, very sad things happen in families—divorce, death, illness. Unfortunately, some members decide it's all their fault.

If only, Dad may think, I hadn't let Jane use the car, she wouldn't have been in an accident with a drunk driver.

If only you hadn't argued with your parents, maybe they wouldn't be getting a divorce.

If only you hadn't wished your brother would drop dead, he wouldn't have died of leukemia.

These thoughts are not based on reality, but on an internal voice that bullies you and pushes you toward guilt.

You now have a need to punish yourself. You are obsessed with the fantasy you were so powerful that you caused your parents to divorce, your brother to die, or whatever tragedy befell the family.

Perhaps when you feel especially guilty, you run to the

refrigerator and find something to eat. While you are eating, the guilt is eased—but only for a short time.

Unless you get help to realize that you are *not* guilty of causing the family tragedy, you may well become a compulsive eater.

Try this exercise to see if you are on your way to compulsive eating behavior. Have a dialogue with yourself:

Me: What's happening?

Myself: I can't stand my parents' divorce. I want them to reassure me, tell me it's not my fault. I need a hug. I'm going to get some ice cream.

Me: What do you think the ice cream will do?

Myself: Nobody's here. I'm lonely, scared, and guilty. At least the ice cream can't hurt me, and besides it tastes good.

Me: Is ice cream able to give you a hug?

Myself: You've got a weird sense of humor.

Me: Well, *can* it give you a hug?

Myself: No.

Me: Can it make your unhappiness go away?

Myself: No.

You should realize from this dialogue that food won't give you what you really want; it's not the answer. Find another activity, if possible. Read a book, call a friend, take a bubble bath.

Mark

Mark and June were the children of parents who worked in professions they didn't like. When they came home at night, the father was often angry and blamed Mark, the elder, for anything that displeased him. June acted out her anger daily, but Mark was the target. It was always his fault.

Little by little Mark began to look to food for comfort. Cake, ice cream, and sweets were abundant in the house. His mother quit cooking when her children reached the age of twelve and filled the cupboards and freezer with fast foods.

One day, June tried to run away, and Mark blamed himself for not having watched her carefully enough. His sister was *fifteen* years old at the time.

Mark's eating increased. Outwardly, he spoke quietly and rationally. He never let his anger surface. Instead, he ate.

By the time Mark went to college, he was close to 200 pounds. He huffed and puffed when he walked, took no exercise, and ate while studying most of the time. After a while, Mark forgot the real reason, his feeling of guilt, for eating. It had become compulsive behavior.

He didn't like being fat. He wanted to diet, but if he ate one wrong food in the morning, he'd tell himself, "It's no use going on today. I'll start dieting tomorrow." Then he'd spend the day eating as much as he could, because he "knew" he couldn't do it the next day.

The next day, the "beginning of the diet" day, he'd look at his enormous stomach and feel disgust. Staring at himself in the mirror, it looked as though he had a tennis ball in each cheek.

It would scare Mark, but not enough: "It's only Tuesday. Exams are coming up. I can't deal with the stress of not eating." Fixing himself a pastry and a hot chocolate, he'd promise himself, "I'll start on the weekend with my diet. I know I can lose fast."

*   *   *

The problem with compulsive eating is that we spend our lives not in the present, but in the future. We picture ourselves as thin *some day.* We tell ourselves the food deprivation will be worth it.

If we actually reach our desired weight, we then compulsively worry if we're gaining again, and once more focus on the future. We never enjoy the present.

Getting rid of our compulsion requires getting rid of our obsession with the future. We need to think about today, about now. We don't need to rush through our lives, gobbling food, hurrying through our days, always looking for something that may never come.

Do you really need to be thinner to do some of the things you want to do? Looking well is the way you hold yourself, the way you talk, the interesting things you say. People will be attracted to you if you get rid of your anxiety and guilt. Mark's feeling of guilt was not a product of reality.

Being aware of the reason you feel guilt, and seeking help from a support group or a counselor will help you overcome your problem. Compulsive behavior may be the last to go, but it can go if you value yourself and learn to have affection for yourself.

TAKING CHARGE OF YOURSELF

Of course, not all guilt feelings lead to overeating. There are many compulsive behaviors, but they all have one thing in common: The person does not really want to do it, but is *driven* to it.

How can one change the cycle?

One of the most important changes is learning to let go

of the false sense of control. If you are in the grip of compulsive behavior, you think you *have* to do it to gain a measure of control so you can be safe. However, it doesn't work that way. Have you ever felt as if you *should* be able to control how others behave, what happens at school, whether someone likes you, or even how fast a waitress serves you? Once you realize you're not in control of any of those things, you can begin to get your life back. A part of you knows right now, as you read this, that such things are not in your control anyway. You might as well let go and have some fun.

If you hold on to your "control," it takes all your energy—energy you could use for better purposes. Also, if you don't loosen your grip it is very hard to gain love and support from others. You can't be in control and still expect to receive love.

Don't think that giving up the drive for control means giving up. It means just the opposite. You'll have your life back and you'll have won—the compulsion will be gone.

THE ROLE OF ANXIETY

When pushed by compulsions, people are at the mercy of powerful impulses without knowing why or what to do about them. Some feel discomfort and anxiety. Sometimes your body acts out anxieties because it can't face the pain. You may not even be aware you're acting compulsively, so how can you be clear about something lurking in the back of your consciousness?

Most people first recognize their compulsive behavior through an incident. Perhaps incessant shopping has gotten you deeply in debt. If you're a fast driver, perhaps you floored it once too often and crashed into someone.

You wake up in a hospital, and an inner voice tells you that you've done it again, but this time your need to speed has caught up with you. Perhaps a friend points out that you're no fun anymore because you practice piano five hours a day or spend all your time cleaning and rearranging your room. Perhaps you suddenly understand by reading a book (maybe even this one).

Having the problem in the forefront of your consciousness is the first step to self-discovery.

Jane's Summer Party

School was out, and Jane's parents encouraged her to have a pool and barbecue party in the backyard. She invited about twenty friends and had everything ready when they arrived.

The guests swam in the pool, splashing each other, having impromptu races, or lounged on the lawn with Cokes before the barbecue started.

Jane kept busy sweeping the patio, bringing more chips or towels, and generally acting like a neatnik.

Finally a group of boys and girls picked her up and threw her in the pool.

"Hey, Jane—you're supposed to have fun. What's the matter?" they shouted.

As Jane came spluttering to the top, it struck her. Why *did* she constantly straighten everything up? She didn't want to. She felt she had to do it, or something bad would happen to her.

Suddenly, Jane realized none of her friends behaved this way. They just enjoyed themselves. She decided she'd find a way to quit her compulsive behavior. She was at the beginning of self-discovery.

THINGS GET WORSE BEFORE THEY GET BETTER

Now that you're on the road to self-discovery and in the process of giving up compulsive behavior, you may feel as if something has been taken away from you.

And something has!

You have taken away whatever compulsion you used to hide your feelings—shopping, eating, cleaning, whatever. There are empty spaces now, and they are slowly being filled with all the hurt you've tried to hide from yourself.

During this time you will probably feel worse. You can't control your feelings, and you don't want to give in to them.

What can you do? The road to recovery is hard, and at this point it is best to look at your feelings and to recognize your pain. You are like a mountain climber taking one careful step after another, knowing the summit is awaiting you.

Diane's Dates

Diane seemed like every girl's dream of how a high school senior should look and act. She had long black hair and huge brown eyes fringed with black lashes. Her long, dark legs helped her win most track and field events for her school. Diane was a favorite with teachers and girlfriends.

However, something was strange with the guys. Although Diane had many dates and even went steady a time or two, her relationships with boyfriends always ended abruptly.

Joan, her best friend, tried to question Diane about it, but the answers were too pat.

"He bored me."

"He's stingy."

"He wanted sex and I didn't."

"All he could talk about was politics."

Diane didn't date only guys from school. She went out with older men, college freshmen, and even junior high kids. She couldn't spend an evening without a date, but usually, after seeing a guy three or four times she'd break up with him.

Yet she was driven to go out, night after night.

One afternoon, Joan called and asked if she'd like to go to a movie that evening.

"I have a date," Diane replied. "I'm sorry."

"With whom?" Joan questioned.

Suddenly, Diane could not remember. She mumbled an excuse and hung up the phone.

"What's happening to me?" she asked herself fearfully.

She threw herself on the bed and visualized a long line of boys whose names or faces she'd forgotten. She began to wonder why she refused to settle for a few boyfriends as the other girls did. Did she think she was too good for them? Too pretty? Too smart? Nothing fit.

"Mom," she called, like a little girl. "I'm scared."

Her mother hurried in and put her arms around Diane, rocking her back and forth.

"Mom," Diane sobbed, "what's wrong with me?"

She poured out her compulsion to date and break up with every boy she met. Diane was feeling the first inklings of awareness.

Her mother fixed some hot chocolate and asked Diane to wash her face and sit with her at their cozy kitchen table. After Diane had talked out her problem, her mother finally wondered aloud if the sudden death of Diane's father when she was four had had anything to do with her compulsive behavior.

Diane looked back in time and saw herself as a tiny girl crying for Daddy. She remembered that Daddy didn't answer her. She was inconsolable and finally angry. Well, she thought, if he doesn't want me, I don't want him.

As she grew, she pushed down the painful memory. When she reached dating age, however, she didn't allow herself to become attached to any guy. Subconsciously she thought, "He might leave me suddenly like Daddy did." So she left first, before she could be hurt, and her anger at her father helped her push the dates away.

During the talk with her mother, Diane realized she needed help to recover from her compulsion, which her mother was happy to provide with love and with therapy. Diane had been out of control for a long time. She still felt tension when she refused dates, and she was often angry.

She did become more aware, and she kept a journal in which she tried to become more in tune with her emerging self. She watched how her compulsions affected her life negatively, and she wrote down her deepest feelings that she had been hiding from herself.

The fantasy that accompanies compulsive behavior is slow to leave, and as it does, feelings of powerlessness and emptiness often take its place. As awareness increases, however, you can begin to trust yourself and your perceptions.

Reexperiencing the beginning of your compulsion may enable you to see the cause and effect in your life. It's hard and heart-wrenching work, but with help you can do it. You can learn to replace old compulsive patterns with healthy new ones.

Remember that compulsive behavior is a misguided

attempt to get rid of pain. You need to work on saying a resounding No to experiences that hurt and replace them with those that make you feel good.

THE HELPING COMPULSION

One of the most time-consuming compulsions is playing the role of caretaker. You've met the type—or perhaps you are one.

When you see someone in trouble, or sad, upset and crying, you rush to help. Not only are you eager to help, but you are convinced that without you your friend cannot survive the crisis.

Your compulsion can take up much time and energy. You become almost as deeply embroiled in your friend's problem and hurt as he is (sometimes even more so). You actually begin to become the person you are attempting to help. When it happens, you have lost control and are of no use. Your compulsion has surrounded you and virtually paralyzed you.

Donna's Mother

Donna, a nineteen-year-old college sophomore, was in the midst of studying for finals. Called to the phone one night, she was informed that her mother had pneumonia and was in the hospital in their hometown.

Donna immediately made reservations for the flight home. On the plane, she started to worry about her mother. Perhaps she should quit college and devote herself to her. She knew her mother could afford to hire nurses, but Donna felt she alone could give her perfect care.

She entered the hospital room and seeing her mother on oxygen, Donna became hysterical.

"Mom," she cried, "just get better! I'll make sure you'll be fine."

Although Donna's mother was weak, she tried to comfort her daughter.

"I have excellent care here," she said. "I'm delighted you came, but in a day or two you must return to school for finals."

"I can't," Donna burst out. "I owe you my life."

This kind of dramatic behavior is out of line with reality. Donna and many compulsives like her think they and they alone can "fix" everything that goes wrong. They want to rescue everyone in trouble.

When rescuing becomes the be-all and end-all of your life, it is destructive behavior. You actively look for negative situations. Let's look at Donna's rescuing behavior. When the doctor called, she began to feel nervous and worried. She wanted to question him, but he ended the conversation too abruptly to suit her.

Interestingly, Donna never asked about her father, who was out of the country on business. *She* was the important one! This was a clue that all was not well with the family. If she had looked back into her childhood, she might have discovered that Mom often asked for help because Dad was so busy. If this was the case, Donna would have been ensnared very early. She had to fix Mom. Only she could do it. Did she ever talk to her father? Perhaps he felt left out. Or he may never have known anything was wrong if his wife needed help but didn't ask.

Donna's compulsive behavior could be worked on. She needed to stand aside and watch the interaction between herself and critical situations. Did she stop to realize that oxygen is generally given to pneumonia patients? No, she thought the worst, "My mother will be an invalid for life. I will quit college and devote my life to her."

Donna's rescuing compulsion came from outside herself; that is, someone called, and her reaction was instantaneous because she had *always* helped.

Are you a rescuer? How would you have reacted when your mother told you to return to college for your final exams? Would you have said, "I see you're well taken care of. When will Dad be home? I'll call, and if you need me when you go home, I'll come back. Besides, finals will be over in four days"—or would you have been horrified at the thought of leaving your mother among strangers when you could help?

If you're a caretaker, dig down into your experiences, and you will find you follow a pattern. You need to be needed; you feel almost "not there" unless you're helping someone. It never occurs to you that your help may be unwanted and intrusive.

If you want to stop your rescuing behavior, step away from yourself and watch your pattern (even write it down). See if you are as essential to those in trouble as you think you are. Realize you need to help yourself most of all. You need to regain lost energy and a sense of self-worth.

This does not mean you cannot comfort others; you can. But it cannot be the only way. You are not all-powerful, and you cannot stop the world's pain.

You deserve a healthy, *happy* life. You'll find you can be of more realistic help to your friends and family if you feel good about yourself.

A part of you probably knows your need to be a rescuer

is an illusion. You have to break the illusion, even though it will hurt. Having spent most of your time as a rescuer, the rest of the time you don't feel quite real. That is the illusion to be broken. Compulsion has taken the place of true feelings.

If you have faced the fact that you are a rescuer, you will also be able face the fact that change is needed.

We are creatures of habit, and any change is difficult. A change from compulsion to freedom is more difficult than most. To get rid of your compulsion you must work at it not sometimes, but daily. Right now, ask yourself:

- Does my compulsion affect friendships?
- Does my compulsion take up too much time?
- Am I afraid if I don't rescue, I will be punished somehow?
- Does leaving my compulsion behind make me feel guilty?
- Is it possible I'll have more fun if I give up my compulsion?
- Do I often feel tired because of the energy I put into my compulsive behavior?

You'll notice that some of your answers are easy, while others make you feel pretty uncomfortable. The latter are the ones you need to work on the most.

Work on yourself. You will need support—a friend, a therapist, or a group to cheer you on in your quest for self-esteem. You will actually reeducate yourself away from guilt, away from feeling bad, and toward a life where the sun shines on you, too. You deserve it.

CHAPTER 3

Degrees and Presentations of Compulsions

Not all compulsions are the same, nor do they take up the same amount of time or energy in your life.

All compulsions have one thing in common—the inability to resist an overwhelming impulse. The extent to which you give in to the impulse is one difference.

Another, far more painful, difference is the *type* of impulse to which you are driven.

FROM PENCIL SHARPENING TO MURDER

When Alma entered second grade, she was thrilled to get her first pencil. She had been bored in first grade with the crayons. She couldn't wait to have a real pencil and learn to write.

As the teacher wrote the letters of the alphabet on the board, Alma eagerly copied them. She wanted her letters to look just like the teacher's. As she concentrated, she pressed too hard and often broke the point of the pencil. She asked to sharpen it so often that the teacher gave her permission to get new pencils from the desk in front of the room.

Although Alma was pleased, she felt guilty about breaking so many points. At the end of the day, she stayed behind and sharpened all the pencils she had used, putting them back on the teacher's desk.

At first, this did not seem compulsive. Rather, it seemed the actions of a conscientious child.

As the years went by, Alma became an excellent student. However, her pencil-sharpening increased exponentially. She irritated her teachers and her fellow students. Moreover, she missed discussions and frequently had to raise her hand to request a second explanation. Since her work was almost always perfect, it was difficult for Alma's teachers to complain of what seemed like a tiny problem. After all, she only wanted her work to look neat.

Do you think that was a correct evaluation of her behavior?

Alma's compulsion, stemming from early childhood, negatively affected her school life because she became an irritant to others.

A sharp pencil was to her a type of (false) security; it made her feel confident in her work. However, she equated neatness with intelligence and good grades.

You may ask why Alma didn't use a pen in her later years at school. Can you guess how her compulsion interfered with such a simple solution?

• Was she punishing herself?

- Was she driven to sharpen pencils?
- What was the underlying purpose of her compulsion?
- What might she have been afraid to admit to herself?
- Do you think there could have been an unspoken command to Alma to remain emotionally a child by refusing to use such a simple adult tool as a pen?

Through her compulsion, Alma was receiving a signal from her unconscious that all was not well. She needed to listen to the message her body-mind attempted to give her. With conscious knowledge of her compulsion, she would be able to get help in therapy and escape the grip of her compulsion.

Some compulsions hurt not only the person who is driven to perform them, but others as well.

In 1992 a gruesome case came to trial, a multiple killer who mutilated his victims, all young boys.

People who knew Jeffrey Dahmer as a child could foresee trouble in his compulsive behavior. Lacking proper care and love, he alternated between depression and rage. He killed small animals as though driven to it. Neighbors noticed his behavior but felt sorry for the lonely child. No one reported his way of "playing." He received no help.

As Dahmer grew older, his angry compulsion took on more and more violent forms. By the time he was stopped by the authorities, he had killed and maimed a number of boys. At the time of his arrest the head of one of his victims was discovered in his refrigerator.

During his trial, it came out that he had been an isolated child whose compulsive behavior to destroy grew and grew. He sat quietly, pale-faced in the courtroom, with no show of emotion.

Had Dahmer been given psychological help, do you think he might have been able to redirect his destructive behavior? We can only wonder. We do know that the worst possible compulsion held Dahmer fast and took the lives of many victims.

Most compulsive people feel alive only when they are in the practice of their compulsion. The rest of the time is pointless.

That is why it is important not to bury real feelings and replace them with compulsion. There is a big difference between real feelings and momentary sensations.

Both the fictional Alma and the real Jeffrey Dahmer had obsessions that originated in childhood. If they had been able to view their compulsions and trace their origins—or been helped to do so—they might well have overcome them.

RITUALS

Much compulsive behavior is done in the form of rituals, which are uncomfortable and cause stress.

Jerry's Play

Jerry had graduated to junior in high school and couldn't wait to take drama with Mr. Reese as one of his electives. He looked forward to the auditions a week before summer vacation ended.

Jerry showed up at the auditorium at the appointed time, along with fifty other students. When it was his turn to read a passage from Shakespeare's *Romeo and Juliet*, he felt sure he had failed, even though the other students applauded loudly.

Mr. Reese said he would notify everyone who had made the class in three days. No one was more surprised than Jerry when a call came from the drama teacher telling him he had won the lead in *Romeo and Juliet*.

As soon as school began, Jerry began to study the part of Romeo daily with Mr. Reese and at home. He had no trouble memorizing, but at home he began a ritual that became absolutely rigid.

First, he hung a sign on his door, "Please do not disturb from 4 to 6 p.m." He chalked a diagram on the floor of his room to simulate the school stage. This way, Jerry told himself, he'd have no trouble remembering the action. He decided to learn all the parts so he would never miss a cue. Although the girl who played Juliet asked him to rehearse with her, he refused except in class.

Jerry began his home rehearsals promptly at 4 p.m. If he made a mistake or forgot a line, he'd nervously begin again from the beginning. Because of his nervousness, he made the same errors over and over again, but he couldn't let go of his ritual.

Actually, he knew every word of the play by the second week of the semester, and he did well in Mr. Reese's class, where he was not in control.

Still, at home he felt he needed his compulsion of putting out his sign, closing his door, and going through his lone rehearsal.

One day a cleaner polished the floor of his room, erasing all his chalk marks. When he saw what had happened, he screamed in frustration and put a lock on his door.

Jerry's parents began to worry. Wasn't he going a bit overboard for a high school play? They decided to ask Mr. Reese about their son's "overdedication," but he assured them Jerry did well in rehearsals and was cooperative.

At home, the ritual continued. If his phone rang and he was interrupted, he started at the beginning again. If he heard children playing outside, he'd slam his window shut and start again. Now his sign stated, "Do not disturb from 4 p.m. until I say so." He refused to come to dinner if his rehearsal had not been word-perfect.

When dress rehearsal finally came, Jerry was certain he knew all his lines, as well as those of the rest of the cast. Mr. Reese smiled at the earnest faces of his students and liked the way they were all prepared.

Halfway through the play, the girl who played Juliet mixed a few words up. No one noticed but Mr. Reese and Jerry. Jerry was completely lost. "We have to start all over now," he groaned.

"Excuse me, Jerry, but I'm in charge here," Mr. Reese called. "Let's move on."

"No way," Jerry screamed. "You don't understand. I do it this way all the time. We have to begin again!"

Mr. Reese, a sensitive teacher, immediately understood that Jerry had a big problem.

He asked Jerry's understudy to take over and took Jerry to his office.

"What's going on?" he asked quietly.

All the pent-up nerves at the core of Jerry's compulsive ritual crumpled. He put his head in his hands and mumbled, "But I have to do it this way."

"Or what will happen?" Mr. Reese asked.

"It has to be right or I start over again," Jerry said, crying openly. "I hate doing it this way, but I can't stop.

If I stop, I'll mess up the play for everyone. You have no idea how hard I worked or how tired I am."

The play went on, with the understudy in the lead. The excitement past, Mr. Reese began to work with Jerry to try to relieve his compulsion. The drama group were very supportive too.

Mr. Reese had the class put on a little psychodrama. Jerry reenacted his behavior at home while another student acted as his conscience. Still others interrupted his ritual, and two students played his worried parents.

The support enabled him to really see his compulsive behavior. But where had it come from? One day he recalled that a baby-sitter he had had for several years always tore up his pictures if he had not used the "right" colors. Trees had to be green and brown, not yellow or red, and the sky had to be blue, not pink. She had made Jerry do every one over and over until it met her standards.

Jerry gradually became aware of himself and some other rituals he had adopted, and after a while was able to drop them. The drama group continued to encourage him.

The following semester, Jerry had the lead in a science fiction play—and rehearsed only at school. The applause and curtain calls were very satisfying, and Jerry was well on the way to recovery from his compulsion.

DRUG ABUSE AND COMPULSIVE BEHAVIOR

We have seen that a compulsive act is done over and over again in order to change a mood. It doesn't matter what the compulsion is. What matters is the change it brings about in you. Momentarily you feel good, whereas before you felt bad.

What does the drug abuser do? He too changes his mood temporarily while on the drug of his choice. He too goes through the same behavior over and over again.

We have also seen how compulsion, like drug use, is often the result of low self-esteem and a feeling of isolation. Both are ways of seeking escape from unhappiness and reality. Can you see how drug use and compulsions are ways of solving problems from the outside rather than deep inside?

There are several differences between addictive behavior and compulsive behavior. In addiction, harmful substances give an instant lift and are life-threatening sooner or later. The compulsive, on the other hand, wants a sense of control, even of power, to drown out his bad feelings about himself.

Despite the differences between compulsion and drug abuse, however, both have in common the *escape from reality*.

Let's look at Carol and Ann, who had similar problems, and see how they handled them.

Carol's Disappointment

Carol, a senior in San Francisco, had her heart set on going to the University of California at Berkeley. At least five of her friends also planned to go, and Carol was excited that she already had a little group to pal around with.

Before doing her homework at night, Carol would go to the gym and work out hard. She pushed herself to the limit, because she thought a perfect body wouldn't hurt when she met interesting boys at college. After her workout, Carol would have dinner and help her mother in the kitchen. She'd been going all day, she would reason, and needed some relaxation. So She'd spend an hour on the phone.

Her homework lay on her desk, untouched. On her way to her room, Carol would notice her parents and younger brother laughing at a sitcom in the living room. She'd check her watch and decide to sit with them until the show ended.

By the time Carol would reach her room, she was in no mood for calculus or chemistry. She'd open the books, leaf through them, do a few problems and stop. Maybe she could do her work the next morning before class. She just couldn't bear the loneliness of her room.

At the end of the year, Carol's Cs and Ds barred her from admission to Berkeley. Her compulsion to be with others, her fear of being alone, even to study, caused her the biggest disappointment of her young life.

Carol never looked inside herself to discover why she needed people around her. Her lack of awareness and her unwillingness to share her fear with anyone kept her locked in. The cycle of compulsion was in full swing. As her friends left for college in the fall, Carol went to work. She continued to live at home, surrounded herself with coworkers, going out with groups of people every night— anything rather than being alone.

Ann's Way Out

Ann came from a low-income family, but her chances of going to a good university were excellent. She was an A student and expected to get a scholarship. Since her parents' divorce Ann had had to care for her four-year-old brother after school because her mother worked as a nurse on the 3-to-11 p.m. shift. Ann became more and more frustrated as her quality time for study evaporated. Her brother had asthma and all too often woke up and required her attention.

Ann often felt that *she* had become the mother and that no one cared for or about her. For the past six months, since her mother had returned to nursing, Ann had struggled to find time to study. Now she felt tired and drained all the time.

She told her friends about her problem, and one of them offered her a pill to make her feel less tired. "Don't worry," she told Ann, "it's a prescription pill. They're for my boyfriend's mother, but he takes a few for me."

"But that's stealing!" Ann objected.

"Do you want to get that scholarship or not?" her friend said. "You grouse about being too tired to study, but you won't help yourself."

Ann swallowed the pill. Within half an hour she became energized. All her tiredness left her. She took care of her brother after school and studied until two in the morning. In fact, she had trouble going to sleep, and lay awake until four o'clock.

The next day she was exhausted. "Oh, that's just in the beginning," her friend said; "you'll get used to it. I have another one, but it'll cost you $5."

"That's my allowance for the week!" Ann wailed.

"Do you want it or not?" Her friend was short.

Ann nodded, paid her, and quickly swallowed the pill.

Once again, Ann felt great. She paid attention in class and had energy to burn. After school, she played ball with her brother, cooked his dinner, and tucked him in for the night before sitting down for a three-hour study session.

"Strange," she thought, "I had no appetite for dinner. Even now I'm not hungry at all."

When her mother came in, Ann fixed her a snack and hustled around the house. Her mother looked surprised.

"Why aren't you in bed?" she asked.

"Mom, I had to study," Ann answered.

"Honey, I loved the surprise tonight, but you need your rest."

"Well, I can't sleep," Ann shouted. "And how am I supposed to rest when I have to take care of Tommy all the time?"

Her mother tiredly bent her head. "We have to pay the rent, eat, and buy clothes, Ann."

"I've heard all that before. You shouldn't have divorced Dad," she burst out.

"But he left us," her mother gently pointed out.

"I don't care. Why can't your sister take Tommy? She lives close by."

"She hasn't been well enough to do it," Ann's mother said. "I'm sorry. I'll try to think of another solution."

At three o'clock in the morning, Ann still wasn't asleep. Her hands shook as she opened her mother's purse and took out a twenty-dollar bill. "Enough for four pills," she thought. "I've got to get that scholarship. Mom has no solution. She's always promising things and never does them."

The next day, she bought four pills from her friend. She hadn't slept in two nights and felt she wouldn't sleep this night either. She just needed to keep moving, to do her work, to clean the house, to read to Tommy, anything but rest.

She became more nervous as days turned into weeks and she continued to take money from her mother to supply her new drug habit.

One Sunday when her mother was home, Ann decided to skip the pill, but she became terribly jittery.

"What is the matter?" her mother asked in alarm.

"You're so edgy. Honey, have you been dieting? You look like you've lost quite a bit of weight."

"Leave me alone," Ann yelled.

"Are you still so tired?" her mother went on hesitantly. Her voice trailed off as she took a very close look at her daughter.

In an even tone, she asked Ann, "Is there something you have to tell me?"

"I've told you all I could," Ann's voice shook and she burst into uncontrollable tears. "No, I'm not tired. I'm never tired anymore." Her tears turned to hideous laughter.

Ann's mother finally realized what the problem was: Her daughter was taking drugs. Ann was admitted to the hospital and spent some time recuperating from very strong diet pills that had been prescribed for someone else.

Ann and her mother had some long talks. The hospital social worker found an affordable day-care center for Tommy. Ann was able to return to her life as a normal and competent student. She was one of the fortunate few, thanks to an alert mother.

The striking similarity between Carol and Ann was that each one needed to do something to avoid a problem. With compulsion as well as drug abuse, there is a desire to stop doing the very thing you are doing.

If a person is compulsive, however, it often goes unnoticed. That behavior is harder to detect than the drug abuser's. The addict's activity is clear to see, and certainly, he or she *knows* that he or she is doing it.

With a compulsion, it is more difficult to notice a harmful behavior because it is so much a part of the person's personality.

Both the drug user and the compulsive person repeat behaviors. When they feel let down or unhappy, they repeat a pattern to alter their mood. Both are constantly seeking to escape real though difficult feelings through momentary relief.

SEXUAL COMPULSION

In today's school society, many students are pressured to have sex—often by the time they are twelve years old. Because the sexually active population is getting younger and younger, it stands to reason that some teenagers have had multiple partners before they graduate from high school.

Is having multiple sex partners a compulsive behavior? Although early sexual activity can lead to a compulsion, having multiple partners is not compulsive in itself.

To understand sexually compulsive people, compare them to drug addicts or alcoholics. The alcoholic drinks until he feels less tension, until alcohol becomes more important than friends, family, or school. Afterward he feels alone and lonely because he has pushed everyone away.

Sexual compulsion is very similar. A sick relationship is substituted for a healthy one. Even the word *relationship* is too much, because the sexually compulsive person has no time to develop love or respect for a partner.

Like an alcoholic or a drug abuser, the sexually compulsive teen retreats further and further from family and friends. Grades drop. Sports go by the wayside. The teen leads a double life, constantly trying to hide the craving for sex.

Such teens perceive themselves as worthless. They are afraid no one would like them if the truth were known. Nevertheless, they believe sex is their most important need. Sex makes not having friends bearable. Compulsive teens try to justify their behavior. They say:

- If I don't have sex, I get tense.
- All my friends do it.
- Whom does it hurt?
- I'm oversexed and need it.

They believe their own lies.

How can you recognize a compulsively sexual person? Everything is exaggerated. There is a predictable cycle of behavior. It begins with thinking about sex all the time, which creates a need for it. The compulsive person has a sort of routine that leads to arousal and even more thinking about it. Constant sexual involvement, whether it is masturbation, intercourse with anyone who is willing, or watching pornography, is part of the routine. The compulsive teenager is unable to stop. Finally, after momentary sexual satisfaction, a profound sadness overcomes the victim caught in this cycle, along with feelings of powerlessness. To stop that, the compulsive cycle begins all over again.

It is as though the teen is obsessively, incessantly searching for excitement. People become mere sexual objects to be used. At times adrenaline speeds up the body's functioning to the point of taking dangerous risks. The compulsive talks often about rituals: compulsive masturbation, or sexual abuse at home, or cruising to find a partner for an hour, or having sex with unknown people in public bathrooms. At times, just talking seems to be enough.

Patrick Carnes, of the Golden Valley Institute for Behavioral Medicine, says, "What we're talking about is a willingness to risk any kind of consequence for a pleasure that gets you so hooked you cannot stop."

Why do otherwise normal teenagers do such things as having constant sex, or anonymous sex, or using vibrators to the point of pain?

Dr. Carnes believes it is a compulsion.

Eli Coleman of the University of Minnesota believes that excessive sexual behavior stems from anxiety.

Such a compulsion may be traced to child abuse, low self-esteem, a lack of love whether real or perceived in childhood, and many other causes.

It is possible to get help and to overcome compulsive sex. Some very successful treatments are modeled on the 12-Step Program for alcohol and drug abuse.

For further information, write or call the following:

Sexaholics Anonymous
P.O. Box 300
Simi Valley, CA 93062
(805) 581-3343

Sex Addicts Anonymous
P.O. Box 3038
Minneapolis, MN 55403
(612) 339-0217

Sex and Love Addicts Anonymous
P.O. Box 119, New Town Branch
Boston, MA 02258

DENIAL

A common compulsion in children is eye-blinking. When a parent asks the child to stop, he or she may reply, "I'm not doing it," denying the nervous habit.

If you are engaged in some behavior that gives you temporary relief, then lets you down, and ultimately makes you repeat it, try to become aware of it. Even if you admit it only to yourself at first, you will be able to start breaking the compulsion.

Shutting down feelings is a way of saying that they don't exist. You deny them—and denial is one way to be trapped into doing things you don't want to do over and over again.

Acting as if everything is fine is denying your real self. It is putting a destructive layer on top of the sad or angry way you feel.

You have the right to be validated for the kind of person you are. You don't need to say that everything is great at home, in school, or with your friends if it isn't so. But remember that denying the truth will make you more unhappy in the long run. It takes courage to look within, to feel the hurt and anger that caused the compulsion in the first place. You can learn to find your own strength, first by facing the truth, and then from support and help available through friends and counselors.

Some places that can help you get started are:

National Self-Help Clearinghouse
33 West 42nd Street
New York, NY 10036
(212) 642-2944

Insight Meditation Society
Pleasant Street

Barre, MA 01005-9701
(508) 355-4378

Hazelden Educational Materials
Pleasant Valley Road
Box 176
Center City, MN 55012-0176
(800) 328-9000

Hazelden offers tapes such as:

Relaxation A Natural High, #1458G
Recovering Self-Esteem/Change, Not
Chance, #1596G

In Canada:

Self-Help Clearinghouse, #215
40 Orchard View Boulevard
Toronto, ON M4R 1B9

Self-Larning/Self-Assessment Corporation
100 Bronson Avenue
Ottawa, ON K1R 6G8

CHAPTER ◇ 4

How Can You Cope with a Compulsive Person?

This book is about compulsion, but not necessarily yours. It is often hard to realize that your parents have problems that you can see but they may not be able to face. The same is true of other family members or friends. You can feel their anguish and see their problems. How can you cope?

JODY'S HOUSE

Jody, a high school freshman, seldom brought friends home. She was afraid they'd make a mess in her mother's perfect house.

Decorated in white and black, with a few touches of color from flower-filled vases, the house never showed a fingerprint, never had a chair out of place or a newspaper on the floor.

Jody's room was furnished all in white. An eyelet bedspread did not invite her to flop down and chat with friends on her white little phone.

Jody was at her desk one evening, trying to write an essay. She was stuck on the opening paragraph and threw several crumpled pieces of paper on the floor.

A knock on the door announced her mother. "You've been up here a long time," she scolded Jody intrusively. "May I ask what all *this* is?" she added, pointing to the floor.

"Mother, please! I'm having trouble getting started on this essay. I'll pick the papers up as soon as I'm done."

"No, you won't, young lady. This house belongs to your father and me. Pick up that mess now, put it in the trash can, and carry it outside where it belongs!" She shut the door and departed.

Exasperated, Jody picked up the papers and carried them downstairs in her little white wastebasket. Her concentration was broken, and she knew she couldn't write the essay then.

The next day, she talked with her teacher and explained the situation at home.

"What does your father say?" the teacher asked.

"He's never home. He travels at least six months of the year. So I get all the blame. Our house should be photographed for an architectural magazine—no one can *live* in it. And now, I can't even do my homework."

"You really need to talk about this when both your parents are at home," her teacher said, "but in the meanwhile, couldn't you do your work at a friend's house?"

"I suppose I could . . . But I can never have anyone over. My mother says everyone is too messy. So I haven't been asked to anyone's house in five years."

Jody's teacher arranged for her to see the school counselor, Mrs. Barrett, who explained to Jody that her mother's behavior was compulsive. When Jody's dad came back from his latest trip, they went together to talk with Mrs. Barrett.

When she spoke about the "evening of the essay," he sighed and admitted his life at home was difficult and only getting worse.

"Your wife needs help, not criticism," Mrs. Barrett warned.

As Jody and her father left the office, he said, "You know, your mother can't get rid of her compulsion alone. She'll need us. I'm going to cut back on my traveling, and I'm going to ask you to do something that's very hard to do. Can you forgive your mother?"

Jody thought for a long time. "I'll try," she finally said, "but Dad, I need to be able to live, too."

"You're right, of course. What do *you* want to do about our problem?"

"Let's first talk *to* Mom. It isn't fair to talk only *about* her."

Jody's father was pleased at his daughter's mature feelings and her honesty.

When they arrived home, Jody's mom opened the door. "I was so worried; you were gone so long," she said.

In the evening they had a family conference. Jody's mother cried off and on. After several hours she admitted she hated "chasing dirt" all day but couldn't help herself.

"Will you let someone else help you?" her husband asked gently.

"I don't need anyone. I'm alone all the time, anyway," her mother cried.

Both Jody and her dad hugged her and promised to be around more. Finally, the mother agreed to see a therapist whom she would choose and who would not be judgmental.

Jody and her father felt relief and a promise of easier times to come.

Do you think Jody's mother could have handled her compulsion alone?

How did Jody take responsibility for herself in an impossible situation at home?

Handling compulsion alone is difficult, if not impossible. Human beings naturally gravitate to one another, so why not avail ourselves of the support and love others are willing to give us?

"Trying it alone," as Jody's mother first suggested, might have worked on a short-term basis, but it might also have driven her into an even deeper compulsion.

Even with therapy, she still had to develop her inner strength and to see her life from within. Her fantasy of "a perfect life equals a perfect house" had to be replaced with the reality of having a husband and a teenage daughter living at home. They too had rights, which included living in comfort, having friends, and being in the midst of a full life.

The recovery of Jody's mother would also become the recovery of the family.

PARENTS WHO HAVE NO TIME

In the modern life-style, many mothers as well as fathers work. This naturally means less time to spend with your parents. In healthy families, of course, an attempt is made to have the hours together be *quality* time. This can make up for a lot.

Some parents, however, take their jobs to a compulsive level. They seem to have no time left for you. How can you cope?

Once again, awareness needs to play a role. Instead of nursing negative thoughts about your parents, try to watch for times when they *are* free and tell them of your concerns.

Kevin and His Professional Mother

Kevin's mother received a promotion in the large firm where she worked. She was thrilled and announced at the dinner table how lucky she was to have two fine, independent, grown-up sons who could take care of themselves. Then she told her husband, John, that he'd probably enjoy having more time to read in the evenings.

"But, Mom," Kevin protested. "We're not grown. Bobby is only ten years old, and I'm twelve."

"It's grown-up enough for you to understand my position," his mother snapped.

"You don't work at night," her husband said. "Whatever do you mean, I'll have more time to read?"

"You just don't want to understand, do you?" she retorted angrily. "I'll leave the house at eight in the morning and return at six in the evening—just time to eat a bite and spend the evening getting my clothes ready for the next day."

"So why do we pay a housekeeper?" John asked. "Can't she get your clothes ready?"

"No one can do as good a job as I can. That's the reason I got a promotion." The subject seemed closed.

Kevin quietly observed his mother over the next few weeks. She talked about nothing but her work at dinner, pointing out that she was irreplaceable, and she didn't know what might happen if she ever had to stay home in an emergency.

The company had been in business for fifty years, Kevin thought. Why is she suddenly so important? It didn't make sense.

After dinner one night, Kevin asked if he could just be with her while she readied her clothes for the next day's work. His mother reluctantly agreed.

To Kevin, the process was an eye-opener. First, his mother picked a powder-blue suit with a white scarf. She chose a purse to match and emptied that day's purse into it. She reached for her makeup and changed it for the next day's. A few moments later, she hung up the blue suit, dumped the contents of the purse in the middle of the bed, and dove back into the closet. Coming out with a pale purple dress, she looked at Kevin and said, "Your staring is driving me crazy. I need to concentrate."

Kevin left the room. His feelings were hurt, and he wondered what difference a blue suit or a purple dress would make to his mother's work.

Kevin was fast asleep by the time his mother had finished arranging her wardrobe for the next day.

His father had read a bedtime story to Bobby, who had started to act very babyish since his mother had no time for him anymore.

Kevin's mother was caught in a cycle of compulsion. She felt she was needed much more at work than by her family.

Kevin and Bobby remembered what a caring mother she had been before. They approached their dad. "What's wrong with Mom? We miss her."

John missed her, too, but he didn't want to add to their misery. He agreed with his sons, however, that Mom seemed compelled to do what she did.

He proposed taking the boys to the beach on Saturday to give his wife a rest, and then take everybody out to dinner.

When Kevin's mother came home that night, she began her usual dreary story about her job. His dad interrupted her by telling her about Saturday's plans.

She grew completely silent.

"What's wrong, Mom?" Kevin asked fearfully.

"Did you even think to check with me?" his mother exploded. "I can't go to dinner Saturday or any night until I'm used to my job."

"Does this mean you can't spend any time with us either?" Kevin braved it out.

"Since you think I have so much time, just when do you think it might be?"

Kevin offered to make breakfast every morning. His dad and Bobby said they'd do the grocery shopping.

Even the housekeeper thought she might be able to take less time off.

"But I don't know how to stop," Kevin's mother finally burst out.

She refused all suggestions.

At last, John found a program that dealt with people who had compulsive problems. He attended with his sons twice a week to try to understand and cope with his wife. One day, to everyone's surprise, Kevin's mother asked to come along. The road to recovery had begun for the mother whose compulsions had begun to affect her family seriously.

Support groups are wonderful ways to help compulsive people. Over 16,000,000 Americans are involved in one sort of support group or another.

If you need a support group because of a compulsive parent, be careful in choosing one. Be sure you know your goals and its goals are the same. Make a list of what you need, and tell your parents why you need help.

Chances are good that you will catch their listening ear, and perhaps the cycle of compulsion in your family will be stopped. Most parents want the best for their children. When they become aware of the needs of their sons and daughters, it may be the very thing that will help them solve their own problems.

COPING WITH TIME

The clock can be a harsh taskmaster if we allow it to control our lives. But "timetables" can work to our advantage if we know how to make them do our bidding.

Marilyn's New Friend

Just as summer vacation ended, a new family moved next door to Marilyn.

Her mother arranged a bouquet of flowers from the garden and took it to the new neighbors as a welcome. When she returned, she told Marilyn the Somners had a daughter, Sheila, who would be in tenth grade with Marilyn.

"I'm afraid I volunteered you to walk her to school on the first day," her mother confessed.

"That's fine, Mom," Marilyn answered. "I'll introduce her to all my friends."

"I told her you'd pick her up at 7:30 day after tomorrow when school begins."

The next day, Marilyn went through her closet and admired the new clothes she and her mother had picked out. She had a hard time deciding which to wear first. Finally, she chose one and hung it on her closet door in readiness.

Getting up early the next day, she showered and dressed. Although she hurried through breakfast, it was 7:35 when she arrived at Sheila's house.

"You're five minutes late," was Sheila's greeting as she frowned at her watch.

"So I am," Marilyn laughed. "Let's at least introduce ourselves."

Sheila smiled and put out her hand. The moment of tension seemed to have disappeared.

The girls talked on their way to school and promised to meet for lunch.

At noon Marilyn and three friends went to the cafeteria. Sheila wasn't there.

"Where could she be?" Marilyn worried.

"You said she has chemistry with Mr. Blake," one of her friends said. "He always keeps his class late. I had him last semester, and he was so involved in teaching, he lost track of time."

When Sheila finally appeared in the cafeteria, her face was red with frustration. She threw her purse on the table and said, "I don't know about this school. Mr. Blake obviously can't tell time."

"But he's a good teacher," Marilyn protested.

"How good can he be if he rambles on and on and makes me late?" Sheila demanded.

The other girls looked uncomfortable. This new friend of Marilyn's had a real chip on her shoulder.

On the way home, Sheila told Marilyn about the importance to her for people to be on time.

"It's like breaking a promise," she said, "if my friends or teachers don't keep their word."

Marilyn thought Sheila was very rigid.

As the weeks went by, Sheila became more and more obsessed with time. She had a fixed schedule of homework, piano practice, and bedtime. She never relaxed and was upset every time her watch showed a few minutes delay.

Marilyn was tiring of her new friend, but decided to ask her why she was so compulsive.

"I can't help myself," Sheila told her. "I just *have* to do it this way."

How do you think Sheila's problem might have started? Use your imagination to make up a background for her.

If you were Marilyn, how would you have handled the situation?

How do you think Sheila felt most of the time?

Where could she have gone for help?

All too often, compulsive people are oblivious to their problem. They can't believe life can be lived any other other way. They are tense and walk around as though blindfolded.

If a good friend confronts the compulsive person, she can take off the blindfold and look at her life in a way she never did before. The key to getting better is always awareness. Without it, the blindfold stays on.

Jim and His Grandmother

Jim was thirteen years old when his grandfather died. Jim and his sister, Susan, missed him a lot. He had been a wonderful man, fun to play with, a good listener, always generous with his time.

Grandmother, on the other hand, was just the opposite. She constantly scurried about, complaining about the weather, her family, her health, and anything else that came her way.

Jim's parents helped Grandmother sell her house and move to an apartment near them. No sooner was she settled than the demands began! She wanted Jim and Susan to run errands for her constantly, although she was quite able to do them herself.

The worst demand for Jim and Susan, however, was her insistence that they visit her every Sunday at eleven o'clock for brunch. "That's the least you children can do," she'd whine. "I used to make brunch at eleven o'clock for your grandfather on Sundays. In honor of his memory, you have to come to me so I won't be alone."

Strangely enough, she didn't invite Jim's parents.

Jim and Susan complained, but their mother and father thought they should go. Grandmother was lonely and getting old.

For months, the children hated Sundays. They had to stay until at least one o'clock, and they felt the whole day was ruined.

When Jim was invited on a weekend camping trip, he decided he had to confront his parents and his grandmother. The next day, as it happened, the whole family was together for dinner.

Jim asked if he could speak about a problem.

"Of course," his father said, "just wait until we're finished eating."

Later, in the living room, Jim looked at his grandmother. "I understand how lonely you must be. Did you know I'm lonely, too?"

She shook her head. "But you're too young! You have friends."

"So do you," Jim retorted, "but when I have time away from school I can't see my friends. You want Susan and me to come *every* Sunday. We can't take the place of Grandfather."

"I've always had brunch at eleven o'clock," she said, "I can't change now. I'm too old."

Jim's parents and Susan were silent. Inwardly, they were proud of Jim for tackling the compulsive woman by himself.

"This has nothing to do with old age," he told his grandmother, "since you always had eleven-o'clock brunch even when you were younger."

"That's the way it *has* to be," she said.

"For you, maybe. For me, a breakfast isn't important enough to *have* to be. I'd come to see you on my own if I weren't forced to be with you at the same time every week."

"I can't help myself. You must come . . . I'm old and alone, and we all miss your grandfather. I've always done it this way and . . ."

Jim interrupted, "I love you, but I hate having to visit you at set times. How about you, Susan?"

Susan nodded miserably.

Jim's father gently asked his mother, "How about it? Let the children come to you freely, of their own accord."

"Thanks, Dad," Susan beamed.

"May I go on the camping trip this weekend?" Jim asked.

His mother gave him permission.

Grandmother sniffed, "Fine, fine. I'll just ask my bridge partners for brunch on Sunday. But I'll tell you all one thing. It *will* be at eleven o'clock."

*   *   *

Jim was strong. He did not accept his grandmother's compulsion. Although he couldn't make her see her own destructive behavior, he was able to deal with her in a kind way. Luckily, he had understanding parents. Jim's grandmother instantly found a way to continue her compulsion by inviting her bridge partners. Since she used her compulsion to keep loneliness away, it didn't matter who served the purpose. She was in a make-believe world in which as long as someone was with her, her aloneness wasn't real.

A compulsion about not wanting to be alone often has as its base a need to control others. People suffering from this compulsion may wonder why relationships are difficult for them. They are always looking for someone who can understand them completely and are disappointed when it doesn't happen. No one can control the inner feelings of others. Beneath the need for control lies fear. Once the fear (of being alone, of not being understood) is confronted, real relationships can be formed without the use of pressure.

If deep feelings are allowed to surface and are faced, the compulsive person is set free to form true friendships instead of fake ones.

THE COMPULSIVE TEACHER

Perhaps one of the hardest things to cope with is a compulsive teacher. As a student, you are trying to get good grades. It's difficult to imagine your confrontation with a teacher, but what can you do if it happens? Let's see how Linda handled a difficult situation.

Linda's Nemesis

Linda's social studies teacher kept a classroom that was always spotless, and taught the same way year after year, never varying her routine. When Linda found out that Miss Smith had been her mother's teacher in high school, Linda wondered when she would retire.

One day, a classmate was having trouble with an essay test. He'd write, then, dissatisfied, shove the paper in his desk and start all over again.

Suddenly Miss Smith pounced on him, hitting the desk with her ruler. Everyone in class jumped, especially Mark.

"What *is* the matter with you?" she screamed. "There is a wastebasket in front of the room. How dare you mess up my class with your papers? I shall now inspect everyone's desk. If I find a paper in it, that person will stay after school and clean the room."

Miss Smith walked rapidly around the room, peering into desks. Linda's desk was crammed full of gum wrappers, pens, bobby pins, and papers.

Miss Smith's fury knew no bounds. Linda tried to tell her that the mess wasn't hers, but the teacher continued her tirade as though Linda hadn't spoken.

Having to stay after school, Linda missed cheerleading practice, which made the coach angry.

By the time she reached home, Linda was exhausted and confused. She told her mother about the day's events. Surprised, her mother said that Miss Smith had been a fabulous teacher. Perhaps, she mused, something had happened in Miss Smith's life to make her so compulsive.

She decided to find out and called Miss Smith to make an appointment for the next day.

When Linda's mother arrived promptly at three o'clock the next day, Miss Smith was waiting for her. Linda was invited to join the conference.

"I was in your class years ago, and I still remember your excellent teaching," Linda's mother began.

Miss Smith looked pleased. "I wish today's young people were different," she said. "I have to push all the time and even clean up after them." Her voice took on a complaining tone.

Linda's mother was silent, waiting for the teacher to continue.

"I'm tired," Miss Smith quavered. "I've worked so long. I've taken care of my mother for the past ten years. She's an invalid. When I come home from work, she makes demands constantly. I get no rest." She was near tears.

"You do too much," Linda's mother said; "can I help?"

"No, thank you." Miss Smith answered in a now soft voice.

"I didn't put that junk in my desk," Linda burst out. "I guess you didn't hear me yesterday."

Miss Smith looked up. "No, I didn't listen to you. I just feel the class must be tidy, so students won't be distracted."

Linda's mother wondered aloud about the custodian's work.

"Oh, he never cleans properly," Miss Smith answered. "If my mother could see the mess in my class, she'd really be disappointed in me."

There it was! Linda and her mother had a long talk on the way home. Miss Smith's standards of cleanliness were directly connected with receiving her mother's approval and love. Since she went home every day to a demanding invalid whose crankiness showed no love, Miss Smith turned to compulsive behavior to change her mood. She acted in a way she thought her mother could approve of—and maybe she could earn love.

You cannot alter compulsive behavior unless the person wants to do so. Certainly, as a student, you are not in a position to "help" a teacher. You can, however, be kind and understanding. If these people could stop cleaning, or screaming, or making ridiculous rules, they would.

If a teacher's compulsion interferes with your grades, however, speak to your parents or the school counselor. Try not to blame, but *do* show your concern.

Your teacher is suffering a great deal. Perhaps you can ask for a change of class. If people in your school realize a teacher is behaving in a compulsive way, they might be able to approach that person more easily.

CAN YOU LIVE WITH IRRATIONAL RULES?

Can you stand being around a coach who is never satisfied with an athlete's performance, or a principal who forbids talking while passing from one class to another?

These are people have a need to be in control. Their self-esteem, they think, is on the line. In fact, their self-esteem is low.

Most people suffering from compulsions don't know that their rules, both for themselves and others, are impossible to follow. They are in a state of *denial*.

Denial is involved again when someone tells you he is not acting irrationally, but for the good of others. A new principal insists that it is more efficient to change classes in absolute silence.

What does it do to you, the victim? It confuses you. Maybe he's right, maybe these rules are good for the school. Maybe he's just strict. Now you are not sure which is reality. You know you've always come to class on time while talking to your friends on the way. The no-talking rule really doesn't make you or others faster.

Perhaps you can join student council and tactfully approach the principal with *your* reality and that of other members. Be prepared, because denial is not always readily recognized. The principal may insist his rules are healthy and normal.

Remember, if the principal is in a state of denial, help from outside will be needed. Explain the situation to your parents and the PTA president (with your parents), and write letters along with your fellow students to the principal or the school paper.

If enough people realize that control rather than education is the goal of your principal, he may be confronted and perhaps get the help he needs to overcome his compulsive control pattern.

CHAPTER 5

Hope and Help for Compulsive Teens

The very first thing you need to do is to discover what makes you feel worthwhile and who is supportive. You must not be alone in your struggle to overcome your destructive behavior pattern.

It is almost impossible to overcome compulsive behavior by yourself. If you say, "I can do it alone," chances are excellent that you'll not only continue your compulsion, but add new ones to your already overwrought emotions.

Don't turn away people who want to help you. You need friends. You've already been too hard on yourself. Remember, compulsions are first born of feelings of isolation. There are also feelings of fear and hostility. Compulsions do not aim at satisfaction, but at safety, because anxiety lurks behind them. You seek either affection or power or both from compulsive behavior.

You are caught in a series of conflicts. You may be

aware of some of them, but not of others. Perhaps you're a little envious of friends whose lives seem to flow along smoothly. You may be right in some cases, but appearances can be deceptive. The people you envy may be incapable of really facing a conflict or trying to resolve it; they may have merely drifted or been swayed by immediate advantage.

If you let yourself experience conflicts consciously, it may be painful, but you'll find it an invaluable asset. The more you face your own conflicts and look for solutions, the more inner freedom and strength you'll gain.

As you begin to realize the harm compulsive conflicts cause, you'll have a need to resolve them. You can't do it with willpower alone; nor can you do it by avoidance. The best method is to change the conditions that brought out the compulsion. It is not enough just to see your basic conflicts.

Of course, insight may bring relief as you begin to see a reason for your troubles. But you cannot yet apply it to life.

You will need help in understanding how your compulsions work in detail—how they interfere with one another, how they stop you from winning a game or succeeding in competition. You'll learn how you vacillate between being too strict with yourself and too lenient: One part of you wants to forgive, while the other condemns you.

With help from a support group, a therapist, or a counselor, you can come to realize that your conflicts *can be* resolved. You must assume responsibility for yourself, feel yourself to be the active force in your life, capable of making decisions and taking the consequences. Along with this go understanding and acceptance of responsibility to others.

After hard work, you will find yourself able to be spontaneous. You'll have an awareness and a feeling of aliveness whether in respect to love or hate, happiness or sadness, fear or desire.

Moreover, you'll have the capacity to express yourself.

CONQUERING GUILT AND FEAR

Many people have feelings of guilt associated with compulsions. An example is a girl who was told by an eye doctor that in a few years she'd probably become blind. She was devastated. She liked to read, to play, and to watch everything the world had to offer.

Her mother took her to another doctor, who was shocked at the diagnosis. "Your eyes are perfectly healthy," he said, "but you do need glasses."

Although the girl was relieved, she became obsessed with her vision. She got in the habit of putting her glasses on and off time after time. If she closed her eyes for a minisecond and opened them, would she still be able to see?

She was very careful not to be caught. She felt guilty about her compulsion.

The girl's guilt arose partly from fear that her mother's anger at her behavior might spoil their relationship. The more she worried, the more deeply she moved into her compulsion. You can see guilt is related to fear. When you ask yourself what you have done to feel so guilty, usually your answer turns to fear of the consequences of your action.

Your fears when expressed as guilt lie buried and unconscious. They are unacknowledged, but they still control your life, just as you try to control the fears through compulsive behavior.

Following are some common fears that lead to guilt, and vice versa:

- Fear of not having control over friends and family
- Fear of wanting
- Fear of your feelings
- Fear of rejection
- Fear of knowing yourself
- Fear of making a mistake
- Fear of failure (The guilt says, "I must be at fault.")
- Fear of success (The guilt says, "How can I do so well when my sister is doing poorly?")

You probably shy away from your fears because of your guilt—you think it's wrong to be afraid, so you deny it.

Psychiatrist David Viscott says, "In our relationships, what we fear is the pain that some emotions might create. The key to facing that fear, which raises our protections and blocks our intent to learn, is seeing pain in a new light and overcoming our fear of it."

What are the pains people are afraid of? Unhappiness, grief, anger, worry, disappointment, and sadness. Such pains are kept inside without blaming anyone else. That can leave you open and unprotected. Your pain may take physical form: stomachache, a stinging in the eyes, or a lump in the throat. If you let go, the physical sensation may come out as tears. To get rid of guilt, which causes fear, which causes pain, open up to it.

Imagine if you'd never taken the risk of walking because of fear of falling. You'd never have learned to walk! Remember learning to swim, to skate, or to ride a bike. In each case you overcame your fear of pain by risking.

It is the same with your emotions. For example, your

best friend forgets you on his Christmas list, a classmate fails to say hello, your date tells you he or she can't make it, your parents are upset with you. You are hurt.

Avoiding pain, fear, and guilt will stop your awareness. And as we have seen, awareness is the key to overcoming compulsions stemming from all of the above.

If you repress your feelings, they won't just go away. They will come out somewhere. You may come home and kick your cat, because now anger has entered your denial of your feelings.

Pain, fear, and guilt are kept within the body. They won't go away until they are faced. If you are filled with such emotions but don't let them out, you'll become depressed and have even greater pain and guilt.

Overcoming fear and guilt takes a long time. First of all, become aware of it. Talk about it. Respect it. Test your fear and guilt.

Suppose you live near a magnificent beach with gigantic waves. You know exactly how close you can go without getting hurt. Your friends think you're a scaredy-cat and laugh at you as they dive into the waves and ride the surf. They try to get you to join them, asking why you won't go in.

"I'm just no good," you answer, "and I'm not athletic, either."

"What are you afraid of?"

"I might drown or not be able to breathe," you answer.

"Why do you think that?"

"Well, I almost died in a swimming pool when I was little. Everybody was splashing and making waves. Water got in my nose and mouth. I thought I was drowning."

"I can understand that," your friend says.

"So can I," you laugh, "maybe it has nothing to do with whether I'm an athlete or not."

Now you have gained self-respect, and you may try to join your friends *even though you are still afraid.* Communication is an important factor in overcoming fear, pain, and guilt. To overcome guilt, remember that you cannot meet everyone's expectations. If you give in all the time in order to be liked, you are giving yourself up. One of the negative consequences may be compulsive behavior—living a highly structured life in which you run to please everyone. You need not feel guilty about not being everything to everyone, nor about not living up to others' expectations. Guilt is destructive.

Many people carry useless guilt and pain around with them for years. You don't have to do that because now you realize that guilt needs to be resolved or you may end up with fear, hate, and revenge. If you cling to guilt, you end up punishing yourself.

You need courage and strength to overcome your compulsive guilt. See it as a positive warning to get help so you can change. Pain and guilt are real and can't be wished out of existence. You must be willing to know them as your own. Once you've done this and learned from them, you are free to forgive (especially yourself) and let go forever.

In the words of Miguel de Cervantes:

"Love not what you are, but what you may become."

A SUPPORT SYSTEM

It is crucial to have someone to lean on when you are trying to end compulsive behavior. As you recover, remember you leaned on the compulsive behavior for years and it was there when you needed it. But that kind of support was fantasy, not real.

You need to create a support system, finding out what supports you and making it a regular part of your daily life.

You may need a therapist. Both you and your parents may wish to speak with several on the phone before you meet with them. It is important to find someone whom you can trust and feel comfortable with. Sometimes, it takes a while to find the right person, but it is worth the effort.

Another part of your support group should be trusted friends who are willing to go with you on your road to recovery. It may be just one friend who will stick by you.

During your recovery, there will be times when you backslide. Then you'll need your support group. You might want to keep handy the phone numbers of friends who are seeing you through.

You may say that you can't always take from your friends. You are right. Watch for opportunities to give while receiving. If you use your friends for support and give nothing in return, your self-esteem will fall again.

YOU ARE NOT ALONE

Important research is being done for compulsive people. It is estimated that five million people in the United States alone suffer from compulsive-obsessive thoughts. A story was reported about a woman who had a new baby.[1] She loved him with all her might, but she constantly had frightening thoughts. Wherever she saw a knife or a pair of scissors, she thought, "I want to kill my baby!"

Unable to understand how such a thing could happen to her, she sought help. A doctor at the University of California in Los Angeles photographed her brain, using a

[1] Los Angeles *Times*, September 16, 1992.

PET scanner. He was amazed to find overworked circuits in her brain, in the cortex just above the eyes.

The patient was treated with medications and behavior therapy. She was able to confront her terror and find the source of it. She was asked to spend time at home with scissors or a knife lying nearby. Gradually she began to get used to them, and they no longer caused thoughts of killing her child. Ten weeks later, the psychiatrist again took pictures of her brain. It had settled down.

In some cases the cause of compulsive thoughts is not found right away, but through behavior therapy the patient's brain activity improves.

Your desire is to rid yourself of compulsive behavior and to be made whole again. You want to experience life to its fullest. As you let your compulsions go, you may realize that you are not tied to your past forever.

Individual power is in each of us. It can be drawn on whenever we wish. Making use of it may be a struggle requiring new learning, or it may be an equally difficult struggle to unlearn what is stopping your growth. Realize that recovery takes time. Don't try to accomplish all your goals in one day.

Meister Eckart, a Christian philosopher of the 13th century, wrote, "The shell must be cracked apart if what is in it is to come out, for if you want to know the kernel you must break the shell."

You, too, can break your shell of compulsion and find yourself, the kernel, to be a good and wonderful person free of fear, ready to embrace life.

COMMUNICATION

One of the most difficult, yet essential, parts of living as a healthy human being among other human beings is the ability to communicate. No one can know you unless you are willing to reveal through your words and actions who you are. You must be constantly engaged in talking so your friends and family can understand your ever-changing self. The alternative is confusion, anxiety, and aloneness.

Communication is not simple. The most important aspect is knowing exactly what you want to say. Vagueness leads to fear and insecurity. Listen to the words you speak and those spoken to you. Try to find language that is not only precise, but the least threatening.

You may want to give the person to whom you are talking the big picture about your compulsion without going into detail. Still, you know the details of your behavior bother you the most.

Elie Wiesel wrote in his book *Souls On Fire*, "But where was I to start? The world is so vast, I shall start with the country I know best, my own. But my country is so very large. I had better start with my town. But my town, too, is large. I had best start with my street. No: my home. No: my family. Never mind, I shall start with myself."

FREE YOURSELF

To become free of your compulsive behavior, first accept the emotional pain as an inevitable fact of life. It is a stimulus for change!

It doesn't mean you ask for pain, but it is necessary when you are experiencing pain to ask yourself, "What is this about?" "How can I learn from it?" "How can I change my response from one of suffering to coping with it?"

You will discover the true reason for your pain when

you deal honestly with it. Your awareness will help you overcome it.

Don't blame someone else for your behavior, or deny it, because it is bound to resurface.

Above all, don't let fear paralyze you, because if you hold on to your compulsion it drains your energy and saps your enjoyment of life.

You have already had the courage to find out some ways of coping with compulsive behavior. Use what you know as an alert to action and to growth.

The American poet and religious writer Thomas Merton wrote:

"First of all, although men have a common destiny, each individual also has to work out his own personal salvation for himself in fear and trembling. We can help one another to find the meaning of life no doubt. But in the last analysis, the individual person is responsible for living his own life and for 'finding himself'. If he persists in shifting his responsibility to someone else, he fails to find out the meaning of his own existence. You cannot tell me who I am, and I cannot tell you who you are. If you do not know your own identity, who is going to identify you?"

Further Reading

BOOKS

Borysenco, Joan. *Guilt Is the Teacher; Love Is the Lesson*. New York: Warner Books, 1990.

Buscaglia, Leo. *Personhood: The Art of Being Fully Human*. New York: Ballantine, 1982.

Carnes, Patrick. *Out of the Shadows: Understanding Sexual Addiction*. Minneapolis: CompCare Publications, 1983.

Fishel, Ruth. *The Journey Within; A Spiritual Path to Recovery*. Pompano Beach: Health Communications, 1987.

Horney, Karen. *Our Inner Conflicts*. New York: W.W. Norton, 1979.

Lakin, Joan, and Whiting, Caroline. *Compulsions: How to Stop Doing What You Don't Want to Do*. New York: Price Stern Sloan, 1991.

Levine, Stephen. *A Gradual Awakening*. New York: Anchor Books, Doubleday, 1979.

Machlowits, Marilyn. *Workaholics*. New York: New American Library, 1980.

Paul, Jordon, and Paul, Margaret. *Do I Have to Give Up Me to Be Loved by You?* Minneapolis: CompCare Publications, 1983.

Rosellini, Gayle. *Stinking Thinking*. Center City, MN: Hazelden, 1985.

Roth, Geneen. *Breaking Free from Compulsive Eating*. Indianapolis: Bobbs-Merrill Co., 1984.

Washton, Arnold, and Boundy, Donna. *Willpower's Not Enough*. New York: Harper & Row, 1989.

ARTICLES

"Addictions: Diseases of Pleasure." *Harper's Bazaar*, February 1991.

Blau, Melinda. "No Life to Live." *SIRS Mental Health*, 1990, 57–61.

Dolan, Barbara. "Do People Get Hooked on Sex?" *SIRS Sexuality*, 1990, #49.

Hathaway, Bruce. "Running to Ruin." *Psychology Today*, July 1984, 14–15.

Levine, Art. "America's Addiction to Addictions." *U.S. News & World Report*, February 5, 1990, 62–63.

McBee, Susanna. "A Call to Tame the Genie of Teen Sex." *U.S. News & World Report*, December 22, 1986, 8.

Nakken, Craig. "The Addictive Personality: Roots, Rituals, and Recovery." *Hazelden Educational Materials*, February, 1988.

Perry, Susan. "Recognizing Everyday Addictions." *Current Health*, May 3, 1990, 20–23.

"Of Jungle Juice and Getting Loose: The Timeless Ritual of Teenage Sex." *Utne Reader, 40*, July/August 1990.

Index